MARRIAGE AS GOD INTENDED

Marriage As God Intended

Selwyn Hughes

KINGSWAY PUBLICATIONS
EASTBOURNE

ISBN 0 86065 212 2

Unless otherwise indicated, biblical quotations are from
the Authorized Version (crown copyright)

NIV = New International Version
© New York International Bible Society 1978

TLB = The Living Bible
© Tyndale House Publishers 1971

AMP. = The Amplified Bible
© Zondervan Publishing House 1965

PHILLIPS = The New Testament in Modern English
© J. B. Phillips 1958

NASB = New American Standard Bible
© The Lockman Foundation 1960, 1962, 1963,
1968, 1971, 1972, 1973

Names have been changed to protect confidentiality

Front cover photo: Tony Stone Photolibrary—London

Printed in Great Britain for
KINGSWAY PUBLICATIONS LTD
Lottbridge Drove, Eastbourne, E. Sussex BN23 6NT by
Richard Clay (The Chaucer Press) Ltd, Bungay, Suffolk.
Typeset by Nuprint Services Ltd, Harpenden, Herts.

CONTENTS

A PERSONAL NOTE
FROM THE AUTHOR

In 1951 Enid and I committed ourselves to each other in a public marriage ceremony at a little church in the beautiful town of Helston, Cornwall. In the presence of God, and surrounded by our families, we promised to live together until one of us should die, no matter what might happen in between. We made that solemn promise in the name of Jesus Christ, whom we loved and served.

We had been married over thirty years, and during that time we have shared both joy and sorrow, poverty and plenty, sickness and health. We have no reason to believe that the future will not contain the same kind of pain and pleasure that we have known in the past, but we are both convinced that the commitment we made to each other on our wedding day is as important to us now as the hour in which it was first made.

At one stage, our marriage ran into serious difficulties. My work as a minister and an evangelist took me to many different parts of the world, which meant that I spent long and frequent periods away from home. It was during this time that the glow left our marriage, and I knew that the fault was mine. One memorable day I began to re-examine my priorities and, after a time of deep heart-searching, I came to see that my role as minister and evangelist was secondary to that of husband and father. In coming to this

conclusion I drew largely upon the principles contained in
the Scriptures. And, sure enough, as I began to implement
these principles in our marriage, it was not long before the
glow returned.

The same biblical principles which I used to rebuild my
own marriage, I began to share with others who were
experiencing marital difficulties and disharmony. They
worked for them in the same way that they worked for
me. Eventually these principles were put into the form of
a course on the subject of *Successful Family Living,* and
were presented to thousands of families in the British
Isles. At present they are also shared with groups of
committed Christians who are training to be marriage
guidance counsellors. I hope that, as you explore the
biblical principles which undergird that most precious
institution of holy matrimony, you will discover how your
own marriage can be rebuilt or reinforced.

1

WHAT'S HAPPENING TO MARRIAGE?

George and Sarah came into the counselling room looking extremely troubled and upset. I knew why they were there because they had previously written to me explaining that they were having 'some serious marital and family problems'. George had hardly sat down before he blurted out, 'Can you help us become a happy family once again? A few weeks ago we realized that we had fallen out of love with one another, and nothing we do seems to remedy the problem. Our children have become unruly and rebellious, and want nothing to do with Christianity and the church. Our family life is breaking up . . . and we can't find any real answers.'

George and Sarah, it seemed, had been growing apart in their marriage for some months. Both were committed Christians, but it was obvious that their spiritual life, as well as their family life, was at a low ebb. There were frequent arguments and rows; the children, a boy aged 15 and a girl aged 16, positively refused to go to church; and they had lost all sense of family unity. As George put it, 'Things are not quite bad enough yet for a divorce, but they are not good enough to be truly called a marriage.'

Fortunately, George and Sarah were willing to undergo some in-depth marital counselling, and after a few months of working with them on their problems, they came to love each other again, and began to build a more meaningful and secure marriage. There was little I could do to help the children, however, as they refused to come for counselling, but as far as George and Sarah were concerned I was greatly encouraged.

George and Sarah are not alone in experiencing deep marital problems. Almost every day I hear of a Christian couple who are either separating or seeking a divorce. And that, to me, is one of the most alarming trends in the Christian church today.

Marriage in trouble

Whether we look at it from a Christian or a non-Christian viewpoint, the institution of marriage is in serious trouble. Ferdinand Lunberg in his book *The Coming World Transformation* predicts that 'the family is near the point of extinction'. William Wolf, a sociologist, claims: 'The family is dead, except for the first year or two of child-raising. This will be its only function.'

Alvin Toffler in his startling book *Future Shock,* in which he looks at the way things might be in the near future, says, 'As conventional marriage proves itself less and less capable of delivering on its promise of lifelong love, we can anticipate open public acceptance of temporary marriages.' He suggests that in the foreseeable future there will be an apprenticeship period for people contemplating marriage, after which there will be an option to either renew or cancel the marriage contract with specially-trained, government-financed foster parents ready to take over the children of dissolved marriages. If present trends continue (according to Toffler) we may well pick up a newspaper in the not too distant future and read an advertisement such as this:

Why let parenthood tie you down? Let us raise your infant into a responsible, successful adult. Professional family unit offers father, age 39; mother, 36; grandmother, 67; uncle and aunt, both 30; live-in, hold part-time local employment. Four-child unit has opening for one, aged 6-8. Regulated diet exceeds required standard. All adults certified in child development and management. Biological parents permitted frequent visits. Telephone contact allowed. Child may spend summer holidays with biological parents. Religion, art and music encouraged by special arrangement. Five-year contract minimum. Write for further details.

Unbelievable? Maybe—but unless something dramatic takes place to reverse the present trends in today's society, this may well happen before we get very far into the next century.

But perhaps the ultimate depth of pessimism, as expressed by those who study the trends in today's society, is that of Nathan Ackerman. 'I am a psychiatrist who has devoted a lifetime to studying emotional problems in families. I have pioneered in the area of family therapy, and from where I sit the picture of marriage and the family in present society is a gloomy one. Family life seems to be cracking at the seams and an effective mortar is nowhere available.'

There can be no doubt that we are passing through an important turning point in history, when marriage and the family are becoming less and less important. Bianca Jagger spoke for a large proportion of today's young people when she said, 'In our society there is no reason to get married' (*Daily Mail,* 19th April, 1982). In a BBC radio report on family life in the USA it was said: 'In the United States marriage breakdown is now growing to such an extent that serious concern is expressed as to the whole structure of society. The broken family will soon be the normal family.'

History records, however, that no nation can survive

the disintegration of its home life. One of the factors in the downfall of the Grecian and Roman Empires was the break-up of a meaningful home and family life.

The real problem, of course, lies not so much with the institution of marriage but with the individuals who live within it. Richard Lessor, a marriage guidance counsellor, writes, 'In the 20th century it is not so much a matter of marriage having been tried and found wanting. Marriage is largely untried. The tendency with couples today who hit troubles in their marriage is to bail out and seek refuge in separation or divorce.'

Why marriages break up

What are some of the reasons for this dismal state of affairs? Some time ago I began to look into why one out of every three marriages in Great Britain fail (in the United States it is two out of every three) and I discovered that there were several identifiable factors which I shall now examine.

1. Society's increasing acceptance of temporary marriages

At one time society viewed a married couple who were not living together or divorced with a good deal of displeasure and suspicion. Not any more. A cartoon in a newspaper pictured a minister performing a wedding, and instead of the usual 'Till death us do part', he said, 'Till divorce us do part.' And this is not entirely unreal, for as Dr Carl Rogers says in his book, *Becoming Partners: Marriage and its Alternatives*:

> We are living in an uncertain age and the institution of marriage is most assuredly in an uncertain state...people are groping, more or less blindly, to find alternatives to marriage ...serial monogamy (with one divorce after another)...new divorce laws which do away with the concept of guilt—these

are all gropings toward some new form of man-woman relationship for the future.

I referred earlier to Alvin Toffler who has been described as 'the greatest social prophet of this century'. He claims that everything in this century is moving with such increasing speed that it becomes impossible to establish any relationship which is both meaningful and enduring. He observed that people today have a 'throw-away mentality'. They not only have throw-away products, but they make throw-away friends, and it is this mentality (he claims) which produces throw-away marriages. I believe Toffler is right: we live in a society which increasingly accepts the concept of a throw-away marriage. Sadly, the external pressure of a society buttressed by strong moral guidelines is no longer with us.

If 30–50% of British Leyland or Ford cars fell apart within the first few years of their manufacture, society would demand a public enquiry. Few voices, however, are raised in concern over the breakdown of marriages, which is fast approaching the 50% breakdown figure.

2. Inadequate preparation for marriage

David Mace, an internationally well-known authority on marriage and family life, says, 'Why do many marriages run into trouble? It is because people don't get the help they need about marriage either before they begin or after they get married.' Generally speaking, young people about to be married do not get adequate preparation either from their parents or from the church. I myself am convinced that if society and the church had given more attention to the subject of pre-marital counselling, we would not now be required to spend so much time in marriage counselling and in struggling to save many marriages from falling apart. Prevention, we are told, is better than cure, and never is that more true than in the area of marriage.

It is sometimes said that in previous centuries marriages tended to stay together without a good deal of pre-marital advice. But we need to remember that past generations had the benefits of a society that saw a broken marriage as a stigma. Today, that is not so. At the time of writing, I have been a minister for thirty-two years, and for most of my ministry, whenever I have been approached by a couple to conduct their wedding service, I have shared with them two principles which I consistently follow.

I tell them that (1) I do not feel free to conduct a wedding ceremony unless the couple agree to complete several sessions of pre-marital counselling, and (2) I reserve the right whether or not to agree to conduct the wedding service until after the first few counselling sessions have been completed. My reason for adopting these principles is this—my approach to pre-marital counselling is not simply to prepare a couple for marriage, but to help them ascertain whether, indeed, they should be married at all. My experience has shown that sometimes during in-depth pre-marital counselling, a couple may decide to either postpone or cancel their wedding plans. I have never been alarmed about this. In my view, a broken engagement is better than a broken marriage. Here is part of a letter I received several years ago from a couple I married in a church in the north of England, of which I was then the minister:

'...and I want to thank you for taking the time to share with us, in those five sessions prior to our wedding, the principles of a successful marriage. Quite honestly, when you told us that you would not conduct our wedding unless we agreed to five sessions of pre-marital counselling, our hearts sank! We both felt there was so much to do in preparing the house for occupation, as well as other things needing attention, that five three-hour sessions would be too much. We were tempted to ask another minister to marry us—someone who would not insist on so many hours of pre-marital counselling. Now, however, we want to thank you for your loving and gentle insistence. The principles you shared with us and the way you prepared us for the problems that could arise in marriage equipped us to deal with things that honestly we would have found difficult and perhaps impossible. When we see so many of our friends and acquaintances who were married around the same time as ourselves, but had no opportunity for in-depth pre-marital counselling and whose marriages are now in serious trouble, we are grateful to God and yourself for the way in which you shared with us. *We are convinced that were it not for those sessions, our marriage would not have survived the storms we have faced in the past few months.'* [Italics mine.]

The need for pre-marital preparation in our society is urgent. Christian churches, as well as some para-church organizations, are in an excellent position to provide a service. It is interesting, as well as sad, to note how some churches treat this matter of pre-marital counselling. Out of a hundred churches of different denominations polled in the south of England a few years ago, only twenty-five said they had a mandatory programme of pre-marital counselling. We should never forget that the church's business is not simply to conduct weddings but to nurture marriages and reinforce family life.

3. Sex before marriage

A third factor in the failure of some of today's marriages is sexual involvement prior to marriage. Several years ago *Redbook,* a Canadian magazine, printed the results of a survey concerning women's sexuality and sexual behaviour on the North American continent. No such research, to my knowledge, has been conducted in the British Isles, but I would imagine the findings would not be greatly different. The report was based on surveys completed by 100,000 women, and indicated that the likelihood of a woman experiencing sexual intercourse prior to marriage had been steadily increasing over the past decade. For example, 69 per cent of the women in this survey, who were married prior to 1966, experienced pre-marital sexual relations. Among those married after 1970, however, the number was 90 per cent. The survey also revealed that a woman who had strong religious convictions was more likely to remain a virgin prior to marriage, but the influence of religion was less inhibiting than might be expected. (Robert and Amy Levin, 'Sexual Pleasure: The Surprising Preferences of 100,000 Women', *Redbook* Magazine.) We have no statistics, of course, for the Christian population as it relates to this matter of sex, but many ministers who conduct in-depth pre-marital counselling sessions tell me that they are deeply concerned at the number of Christian couples who confess to experiencing sexual intercourse during their courtship days.

One minister in the London area who marries, on an average, twenty-five Christian couples a year said that about twenty out of the twenty-five confessed to engaging in pre-marital sex. A Scottish minister told me recently that out of the twenty Christian couples he married in 1981, sixteen of them said they had been sexually intimate.

One of the things I have noticed, in my own counselling experience with hundreds of married couples, is the way in which pre-marital sex undermines the foundation of a marriage. I can think of at least a dozen couples I have seen in the past year whose marriage problems were largely due, not to any of the usual factors such as immaturity, financial pressure, in-law difficulties, but because, during their courtship days, they had engaged in pre-marital sex, and had never dealt effectively with the spiritual principle they had broken. There is no doubt (in my mind at least) that fornication (sexual relationships prior to marriage) undermines the foundation on which a marriage must be built, and unless necessary and important steps are taken to clear up the conflict which the act of fornication creates, then the marriage is wide open to problems.

Paul speaks out strongly against sexual impurity in many of his letters. For example, in 1 Corinthians 6:9–20, he warns that those who continue to practise fornication 'shall not inherit the kingdom of God' (verses 9–10). He adds, 'Now the body is not for fornication, but for the Lord' (verse 13), and that our 'bodies are the members of Christ' (verse 15), and temples of the Holy Spirit who is in us (verse 19). In Galatians 5:19–21, sexual immorality, impurity and sensuality are included in Paul's list of 'the works of the flesh' and 'they which do such things shall not inherit the kingdom of God'. In Ephesians 5:3–12, Paul exhorts the Ephesian Christians not to let sexual immorality or impurity even be named among them (verse 3). An examination of God's word clearly shows that in matters of sex one should wait until marriage.

Many married couples I have counselled have shown great surprise when, during the course of counselling, I ask them about the pattern of their relationship during their courtship days. I do not always do this, of course, but whenever I am involved in dealing with a serious marriage breakdown and the marriage needs to be thoroughly overhauled, I seek to discover whether or not the couple became involved in a sexual relationship prior to marriage. In doing this, I am not attempting to be voyeuristic, but to ascertain if a spiritual principle was broken and whether steps have been taken to put it right. Many couples, I find, have the naïve attitude that even though they were involved in pre-marital sex, now they are married the matter is resolved. But it's not as easy as that. Once a spiritual principle has been violated, it can never be swept under the carpet. It must be dealt with in a proper scriptural manner—by confession and repentance.

Remember the story of the church of Ephesus recorded

for us in the book of Revelation (Revelation 2:1–7)? The church had violated a spiritual principle and had 'left its first love'. Now what did Jesus say? Did he counsel them to recover their first love and then the past would be forgotten? No. Jesus was too wise a counsellor to treat the matter in that way. Guilt which descends upon the human spirit whenever a spiritual principle has been violated can only be dealt with effectively by an act of repentance. It was not enough that the Ephesian church got back their first love. The past had to be properly dealt with, and so Christ commands them to 'repent and return'.

I have advised hundreds of couples, who shared with me that they were guilty of wrong standards in courtship, to confess this to the Lord, ask his forgiveness for the violation and then ask each other for forgiveness. It is a simple procedure, but when done in true humility and genuine repentance, it removes the seeds of disintegration that lie at the base of the marriage. One wife told me, 'I had a nagging doubt in my mind that was there day and night. It was this—I wonder if my husband would have married me if I hadn't allowed him to have sex with me? But once the matter was brought out in an act of repentance and confession and my husband asked for my forgiveness for the sin of fornication, it brought a new atmosphere in our marriage from that very moment. I knew then that if our marriage had not been on a firm footing before—it certainly was now.'

How many marriages, I wonder, struggle along for no other reason than that the matter of pre-marital sex has not been faced and dealt with in a scriptural manner?

4. Changing roles

A further factor in the failure of some of today's marriages is the movement away from fixed marital roles to more fluid roles. William Ledrerer and Donald Jackson, both secular writers, in their book *The Mirages of Marriage*, point out that one of the most destructive elements in a marital relationship is the failure of the marriage partners to identify, determine and mutually assign areas of responsibility—who is responsible for what? Many married couples today live together in a sort of non-leader co-existence. One sociologist says,

> This is a fairly recent occurrence, a more militant outgrowth of the feminist movement. Anthropologists and zoologists tell us that in any given group of human beings or animals, a leader will emerge through election or a power struggle. For the modern liberated husband and wife to agree to a leaderless co-existence is to agree to a life of frustration in which there is no established procedure for resolving problems.

Several researchers in social psychology have designated at least five kinds of 'social power', authority or influence that human beings exercise over each other. Barry E. Collins and Bertram H. Raven, in their book *Group Structure: Attraction, Coalitions, Communication and Power,* say that the first kind of power is that which comes from one person knowing more than another. A person exerts this sort of 'power' when the information or knowledge he controls influences someone else's thinking and behaviour.

The second kind of power comes when a person, being more capable than another, influences the lives of others by his superior ability.

A third kind of power is described as 'coercive reward' power. This exists when a person believes that the one to whom he relates can punish or reward his behaviour.

The fourth power is that which comes from a relationship where one person admires another so highly that he longs to be like him. This is referred to as 'reference' power.

Finally, the fifth form of power is called 'positional' power. This exists when one person accepts a relationship whereby another, because of his position, is allowed to tell him what to do.

When we examine the nature of the husband-wife relationship from the point of view of Scripture, we see that of the five kinds of power listed above, *positional power* is said by the New Testament to belong to the husband. This is the power that is given to a husband by God so that he is able to direct the affairs of the family and be the head of the home and the leader in the relationship. More will be said about this later, but let it be noted that the movement away from clearly identifiable marriage roles, where the husband is the leader, is impeding rather than advancing the cause of marriage.

5. *Romantic love is not enough*

One last cause that contributes to the downfall of marriages is the attempt to build a marriage on nothing more than romantic love. Now let me say at once that a certain amount of romantic love is an important aspect of marriage, especially in the early stages. I shall say more about this later, but, right now, I want to focus on the fact that romantic love, *by itself,* is not a sufficiently strong base on which to build a marriage.

Romantic love has been called 'cardiac-respiratory love'. It is love with an emphasis upon excitement, sensual thrills and palpitations of the heart. One writer says, 'Some people react to the early days of marriage as if there was a lack of oxygen in the vicinity. Ecstasy, day-dreaming, a deep physical yearning and an apparent fever are all indications of this malady.'

Dr James Peterson so effectively describes the danger of attempting to build a marriage on mere romantic love that I am quoting him in full:

First, romance results in such distortions of personality that after marriage the two people can never fulfil the roles that they expect of each other. Second, romance so idealizes marriage and even sex that when the day-to-day experiences of marriage are encountered there must be disillusionment involved. Third, the romantic complex is so short-sighted that the pre-marital relationship is conducted almost entirely on the emotional level and consequently such problems as temperamental or value differences, religious or cultural differences, financial, occupational, or health problems are never considered. Fourth, romance develops such a false ecstasy that there is implied in courtship a promise of a kind of happiness which could never be maintained during the realities of married life. Fifth, romance is such an escape from the negative aspects of personality to the extent that their repression obscures the real person. Later in marriage these negative factors to marital adjustment are bound to appear, and they do so in far greater detail and far more importantly simply because they were not evident earlier. Sixth, people engrossed in romance seem to be prohibited from wise planning for the basic needs of the future even to the point of failing to discuss the significant problems of early marriage.

It is difficult to know how pervasive the romantic fallacy really is. I suspect that it creates the greatest havoc with high school seniors or that half of the population who are married before they are twenty years old. Nevertheless, even in a college or young adult population one constantly finds as a final criterion for marriage the question of being in love. This is due to the distortion of the meaning of a true companionship in marriage by the press, by the magazines, and by cultural impact upon the last two or three generations. The result is that more serious and sober aspects of marital choice and marital expectations are not only neglected but sometimes ridiculed.

Far too many people enter into marriage with little idea of the quality of love that is needed in order to stand up to the tests and difficulties it produces. Whenever I ask a couple about to be married the question: 'Why do you want to get married?' the usual reply is: 'Because we love each other.' Then when I begin to probe as to what kind of

love they are talking about I get some strange and con-
fusing answers. 'Love,' one starry-eyed young woman
told me, 'is cuddling up in bed on a cold night with someone
who turns you on.' One counsellor I know was given this
response when he asked a couple for their definition of
love: 'Love is a feeling you feel when you feel that you are
going to get a feeling you never felt before.'

Many people enter marriage with no more idea of the
type of love that is required than the couple I refer to
above. But marriage cannot be sustained by romantic
love alone. When a couple stand before the altar expressing their marriage vows, there is no assurance that five
years later they will feel the same kind of love they felt as
they walked up the aisle. The possibility of long-range
love hardly occurs to them. The love that survives the
problems of marriage is a love that has in it a degree of
commitment, not just a flush of feeling. And, unfortunately, many people today enter marriage with little or
no realization of the need for a commitment that will
outlast romantic feelings. Sometimes a marriage needs
hard work, and many people in today's society are un-
accustomed to working through problems.

We face a culture which mocks long-term relationships,
despises effort, ridicules discipline and prefers to accumu-
late things rather than develop relationships, and seeks its
own self-centred pleasure at the expense of another's.

The cultural shockwave which is engulfing today's
society is bad enough, but how tragic that it is rapidly
making inroads into the church of Jesus Christ. It is fairly
obvious that the supportive elements of society can no
longer be relied upon. We must turn, therefore, with
renewed faith to the proved and trusted truths of Scripture.
We need to understand how superbly God speaks through
his word to human needs. God has a good deal to say in his
word about how to build a good and happy marriage. And
yours can be a happy one if you will learn to practise the

biblical principles that relate to marriage. Even if only one partner obeys, there can be a tremendous improvement, but if both partners respond then marriage can become, as Luther described it, 'the nearest thing to heaven on earth'.

2

WHO'S IN CHARGE?

'Woe to the house where the hen crows and the cock keeps quiet,' says an old Spanish proverb. It is saying, in other words, that somebody has to be in charge and it had better be the one designed for the task!

Of course, the traditional view of the husband being the leader and the wife the follower is coming under heavy fire in today's society. During the past few months, I have been in close contact with several married couples who are in serious trouble because they are trying to run their marriages on the basis that both of them should be leaders. And, as Billy Graham's wife Ruth once said in an interview, 'If there are two leaders in a marriage then one of them is unnecessary.' We are living in dangerous times when people are tampering with God's principles for marriage, and, quite simply, the issue is this—*unless we heed the helm we will have to heed the rocks*. Fine phrases about liberation, mutual submission, egalitarianism sound good and enlightening, but as far as marriage goes, they are unscriptural, even anti-scriptural.

Whenever I am invited by a couple to help them resolve the problems they are encountering in the area of personal relationships, the first thing I do is to examine their understanding of the biblical roles. Over the years I have been working as a counsellor, I have discovered a very interesting equation: roles determine relationships. Show me a marriage in which the roles are clearly defined, clearly understood and acted upon, and I will show you a marriage where relationships blossom like a beautiful flower.

Now I know, of course, that at this point some will say: 'Roles? What roles?' This is because we are living in a society where marital roles have become greatly blurred. The radical feminist movement has been vigorously and foolishly trying to persuade us that apart from the ability to bear children, there are no differences between men and women, and that those who insist there are have become victims of centuries of oppression.

The Bible, however, is quite clear on this issue of marital roles and addresses it with great clarity and insight. Take, for example, the book of Ephesians. The first three chapters have been described as 'the theological foundation' and the last three chapters, 'the experiential superstructure'. In the second section Paul gives two key words which help us understand the role a man and a woman should follow in marriage. The husband, he says, is the head of the wife and must love his partner as Christ loves the church (Ephesians 5:23, 25). The wife, on the other hand, is to submit herself to her husband in the same way that the church is subject to Christ (Ephesians 5:24). Let's now look a little more closely at these roles.

The husband—a loving leader

Paul in Ephesians makes it quite clear that God has given the husband the responsibility for leadership in the marriage. But note it has to be more than just leadership—it must be *loving* leadership. 'Husbands, love your wives, even as Christ also *loved* the church.' Some husbands I know view leadership in the home in the same way that a drill sergeant surveys his men on the parade ground. He struts up and down in front of his family, barking orders and shouting, 'I'm head of this home.' That's not leadership—that's dictatorship.

Look at the words again, and note this time where I have placed the emphasis: 'Husbands, love your wives, even *as* Christ also loved the church.' And how does Christ handle his relationship with his church? Does he ram biblical truth down our throats? Does he rule us with a rod of iron? Of course not! He is quite firm but gentle; insistent but not strident; unwavering yet compassionate. This is the model which Paul, writing under the inspiration of the Holy Spirit, holds out to every Christian husband— 'Love your wives, even *as* Christ also loved the church.'

I must admit that the first time the truth of these words really dawned on me, I felt deeply incapable and inadequate. I came into marriage thinking my main role was to get my wife to submit to me. Imagine the shock I received when I discovered that my major function was to love my wife *as* Christ loves the church. I remember falling upon my knees and crying out to God in desperation: 'Lord, how can I ever rise to such unattainable heights?' God's word to me in that hour was something I have never forgotten. He said, 'Not only have I lifted the standard to great heights, but I have also provided the power by which you can reach up to it.'

The word God gave me that day, now close on twenty-five years ago, is indelibly imprinted on my memory. Now, whenever I feel inadequate and unable to love my wife in the way that God demands—as Christ loves the church—I simply kneel in his presence, hold up my empty cup beneath the fountain of his love, and he fills it over and over again. No man can love his wife in the way God requires until he bows in the presence of his Master and confesses that he needs divine help. This is something the male ego shrinks from, as it clamours for mastery and independence. Yet, when a man submits to God and confesses his need of divine resources, he creates a climate and an atmosphere within his personality which makes it easy for his wife to submit to him.

Many years ago, when I was a pastor, I set out one afternoon to visit a fine young Christian couple whose marriage ceremony I had conducted about six months before. When I entered the home, my heart sank. It was obvious they had been involved in a violent quarrel, as the wife's body was bruised and bleeding. 'What's happened?' I asked. In between bouts of sobbing and tears, the wife told me that tension had been building up for several weeks, and today things had exploded. And the issue? Headship. The husband was seeking to set up what he thought was scriptural headship in his home, but he had gone about it in such a way that had caused a strong negative reaction in his wife.

In the conversation that followed, I discovered that the wife believed implicitly in the scriptural roles as set out in Ephesians chapter 5. She wanted her husband to be the head. She desired to follow the principles of the Bible. But something was wrong. It surfaced when the husband told me that, try as he would, he could not get his wife to submit to him. At that point I asked him how he saw his role as a leader in the home. This was his reply: 'God has given me the responsibility to run the home and I expect total obedience from my wife in everything I say and do. She has not given me this and I'm afraid it ended today in this squabble.'

It was quite clear from his reply that the young man, sincere Christian though he was, had little idea about true Christian headship. It is my experience and observation that most men's concepts of headship and authority come largely from the natural mind and not from a careful study of the Scriptures. I showed him from the Scriptures the verse to which I have already referred: 'Husbands, love your wives, even as Christ also loved the church.' 'Can you honestly say you can do that without invoking God's resources?' I asked. He was silent for a few moments and then quietly said, 'No.'

After several hours of discussion that young man came to a proper understanding of his role as a leader in his home, and when finally he sank to his knees and confessed his need of divine help in fulfilling the role God had set for him, I knew he was on his way to establishing a successful and meaningful marriage. Later he apologized to his wife for the spiritual hurt and physical violence he had caused her, and when I left them they were sitting together on the sofa holding hands and reading through the fifth chapter of Ephesians.

Some months afterwards, when I talked to the wife and asked her how things were going in her marriage, she told me how impressed she had been with her husband's humility in openly asking for God's help in loving her in the way Christ loves the church. 'For some strange reason,' she said, 'his action produced in me a more responsive and submissive spirit than anything he ever said.' It is something that never ceases to amaze me, and I have been watching it at work for many years now, that whenever a man visibly throws himself on the resources of the Holy Spirit to love his wife in the way Christ loves the church, this produces within him characteristics to which his wife delights to respond. A woman can instinctively tell whether her husband's leadership flows out of his own submission to Christ or develops out of the demands of his own ego. Nothing gives a woman greater security in a marriage than knowing her husband is completely committed to God. A husband's attitude in this matter is tremendously important. Let him assume he is the head because he is in some way superior and his wife will feel greatly threatened. Let him see it as a God-given role, an assigned responsibility, and the whole atmosphere of his marriage will change.

Is man superior?

I am often asked the question: 'If a husband is appointed by God to be the leader in a marriage, does this mean that he is to be regarded as the superior partner?' The answer is no. Both husband and wife are equal in the sight of God. The apostle Peter puts it beautifully when he says, 'Similarly, you husbands should try to understand the wives you live with, honouring them as physically weaker yet equally heirs with you of the grace of life' (1 Peter 3:7 PHILLIPS).

But being equal does not mean that a man and woman have the same function. A husband and wife may be equal spiritually but not functionally. The functional difference has been established by God, and any attempt to change this will produce serious fractures in the marital relationship. It is sometimes very difficult for new Christians, or for that matter, older Christians, to comprehend the difference between spiritual equality and different functional roles. One person, in a question and answer period following a *Family Life* seminar I conducted, asked, 'If according to Galatians 3:28, "there is neither male nor female", how can it be claimed that men and women have different roles?' I replied, 'Because in Galatians 3:28, Paul is not examining respective roles but individual worth. We are all equal spiritually but that does not mean we all have the same functions. And the functional distinction is examined in detail by Paul in Ephesians 5.'

How to love her

We said earlier that the main ministry and role of a husband in marriage is that of a loving leader. He is not only to lead—but to lead by love. I remember asking myself one day many years ago, why does God make such a demand on a husband to love his wife? The answer

came—because to be loved is her greatest need. Byron
put it like this:

> 'Love to a man is a thing apart...
> 'Tis woman's whole existence.'

After marriage a man needs only occasional reminders
that his wife loves him whereas the woman needs constant
reassurance of this fact. As plants need sunshine and
water without which they easily die, a woman needs
constant love and attention if she is to flourish as a woman.
When she is deprived of this she 'wilts on the vine'. Men
are not affected by the lack of love to the same degree that
a woman is. A man deprived of love may throw himself
into his work and find compensation or fulfilment there.
Not so with a woman. If she is deprived of love, she is
shaken to the depths of her personality and will suffer as
no man can comprehend.

What then are some of the ways in which a man goes
about the God-given task of loving his wife? Firstly, he
must *express* his love. Although women are enraptured
with words such as, 'I love you,' or 'You are beautiful,'
they like also to see expression of their husband's love.
The small thoughtful gift that says, 'I thought about you
today'; the telephone call when she is not expecting it; or
just helping her with the housework—cleaning the
windows, vacuuming the rooms or washing the dishes.
Enid, my wife, has often told me that it is not the expected
gifts, such as those given on birthdays or anniversaries,
that mean most to her, but the small, even inexpensive
things I bring home—when not expected. Men, because
they don't need as many reassurances as women in relation
to this matter of love, tend to leave their expressions of it to
the big romantic occasions such as Valentine's Day or
wedding anniversaries. But women are different—they
delight in the little things that mean a lot.

One of the most appreciated expressions of love which a woman delights in receiving from her husband is *tenderness*. A touch of the hand, a pat on the shoulder, a tender word—indeed any act of tenderness moves her to the deepest part of her being.

Another way in which a man ought to go about the God-given task of loving his wife is by sacrificing for her. In every instance of genuine love there is an element of sacrifice—some extra effort, something one goes without, some trouble to attain. Sometimes, when conducting a *Family Life* seminar, I ask the men: when did you last sacrifice yourself for your wife? When did you last give up something you enjoy—such as watching sport on TV—just to please her? There is no point, of course, in sacrificing something simply for the sake of it, but there are times when a husband ought to illustrate to his wife the meaning of the cross, and show by example what it means to die to self. Why does the cross of Christ have such a tremendous drawing and constraining power? It is because the human heart responds in a mysterious way to the sacrifice of another on its behalf. When a man leads his wife by sacrificing himself for her, he touches something deep inside her being which causes her to respond with gladness and delight to his example.

Larry Christenson, a Christian author and writer on the subject of the Christian family, says that when an argument flares up in a marriage it is the husband's place first to humble himself and beg forgiveness for whatever was wrong in his behaviour. This is death to the ego. It may be that his wife's guilt is as great or greater. No matter. His call is to love his wife as Christ loves the church. In the Spirit of Jesus Christ, therefore, determine to forgo your own pleasure, and think of ways in which you can sacrifice yourself for your partner. In doing this, you will not only sanctify yourself, but you will also sanctify your wife. As you are drawn to Christ by reason of his sacrifice for you, so will she be drawn to you by reason of your sacrifice on her behalf. It is the mystery of sacrificial love creating its own response.

A third way in which a man ought to go about the task of loving his wife is by holding her in high esteem. It is a simple psychological fact that if you place a high value on a person and make that person aware of your expectations for them, they tend to become like the person you see them to be. This is especially true with women. 'Treat your wife like a queen,' said one writer, 'and she will tend to act like one.'

Recently I read the story of Johnny Lingo, a Polynesian boy, who fell in love with a girl of the same race who lived on a nearby island. The girl suffered from a deep inferiority complex due to being downgraded by her father. She used to hide behind the banana trees to conceal herself from the gaze of men and women whom she thought regarded her as a social outcast. Johnny Lingo knew her when she was a little girl and remembered her as a person of value and worth. Now that he was a fully grown man, he decided to visit the island and ask for her hand in marriage.

When he met her he was deeply upset by her negative self-image, but it made no difference to his determination to marry her. It was the custom in the islands that when a man asked a father for his daughter's hand in marriage, he bargained with him for a certain number of cows. If a woman was ordinary, he might have to pay only one cow for her. If she was of great worth, and the competition was keen, he might have to pay two or even three cows for her. Women took personal pride in how many cows they were bargained for. Johnny Lingo set out to bargain with her father who, of course, was quite prepared to give her away for only one cow. Johnny offered him eight cows. The father naturally jumped at the offer. When asked later why he did not bargain with his future father-in-law, Johnny replied that he wanted everyone to know, especially his wife, that in his estimation she was worth the highest possible value. A great change came over the girl after that. Her self-esteem soared and as she realized her worth, she took on the dignity and bearing of a girl worth eight cows!

The power a man holds over a woman to either bring out the best in her or demean her is awesome. Aubrey Andelin, in an article in *New Wine* magazine, claims that many women are lured into the women's liberation movement because they have not been treated properly by their husbands. 'Most women,' he says, 'would not give the liberationists a second chance if their men honoured them in the way a woman deserves to be honoured.'

A fourth way in which a man ought to love his wife is by making allowances for her deficiencies and mistakes. We may all know it, but it needs to be said: women, like men, are human and will sometimes make mistakes. They may be late, fail to have dinner ready on time, or present food that is not perfectly cooked. Sometimes they fail to keep the house as neat and tidy as it ought to be, or they may not handle the children wisely. Well, we don't marry angels! I made that remark in a seminar once, and a man came up to me at the end and said, 'I married an angel.' 'What do you mean?' I asked. He replied, 'My wife flies up in the air over the slightest thing!' A man who expects an angel for a wife is being decidedly unrealistic.

Many men I know tend to be extremely critical and harsh when their wives fail in some way or make a mistake. She can do a hundred things right, but let her fail in just one respect and he comes down upon her harshly and bitterly. In an article I once read where women were asked to list the qualities they would best like to see in their husbands, 'allowing for mistakes' came second on the list. The first was 'to be treated as a person and not an object'.

One of the reasons why men find it difficult to allow for their wives' mistakes and failures is due to lack of humility. A man who knows true humility will realize that he himself is imperfect, and this knowledge will temper his judgement when dealing with his wife's failures and mistakes.

Another reason why a man fails to overlook his wife's deficiencies and mistakes is because of a misplaced perspective. Some men look continually at the negative things in their wives and thus overlook the positives.

Once I was counselling a man who was having trouble in his marriage. After he had spent some time underlining the deficiencies in his wife, I asked him to list some of the positive factors about her. 'She hasn't any,' he said. 'Come now,' I replied, 'there must be one or two. What about the way she cooks or the way she looks after the children?' 'Yes,' he admitted grudgingly, 'she is quite good at those things.' Gently I pressed him to give me several other positive qualities, until we reached a list of twelve or so things. I read the list out to him and as I did I sensed a change in his whole attitude. 'I never realized she had so many good qualities,' he said. 'Looks like I've been looking in only one direction.'

Later that man told me that, in focusing on the positive qualities in his wife, he felt a considerable change in his attitudes and feelings towards her. I was not surprised.

It is a scriptural principle that what we focus on greatly affects our attitudes and feelings. *What we think about affects the way we feel and act.* This is why the Bible encourages us in Philippians 4:8 to 'think on these things'. When we focus our thoughts on positive things, we come out with positive feelings. When we focus our thoughts on negative things, we come out with negative feelings. So whenever you are tempted to focus on your wife's mistakes and deficiencies, think also of her positive qualities. You will most likely find that they outweigh the negative ones by a hundred to one.

When a wife makes continual mistakes which create great problems for herself and others, then it becomes the husband's responsibility to teach her how to overcome them. If this instruction is given with kindness and freedom from sarcasm, a woman will usually respond favourably.

A fifth way in which a man ought to love his wife is by encouraging her to share her view of things. Some men feel that leadership means that the husband arbitrarily makes decisions affecting the home without any consultation with his wife. To do so is to deny the reason God gave him his wife in the first place. Generally speaking, a woman tends to see things in detail while a man tends to see things in a wider perspective.

I remember a man telling me once of how one evening he sat on his veranda watching a beautiful sunset. As the sun set in a splash of colour, he said to his wife, 'Isn't that beautiful?' 'Yes,' she murmured, and then was gone. He saw her a few minutes later at the bottom of the garden cutting a white rose from a bush, which she then promptly carried into the kitchen. She placed it in a vase of water and sat there for almost an hour admiring it. 'While I drooled over the glorious sunset,' said the man, 'my wife drooled over a tiny flower.' But that's one of the intriguing differences between a man and a woman—he appreciates the wider perspective, the wife, the smaller and more detailed one. This is a generalization, of course, and, like all generalizations, there are exceptions.

I discovered a long time ago that my wife has an ability to spot details which I frequently overlook. And my decisions were much more soundly based when I learned to consider her viewpoint before making them. Encouraging a wife to share her viewpoint on things does not simply mean tolerating her perspective on things only to go the way you planned originally! It means listening to her sensitively, recognizing that she may provide you with the other half of the wisdom that God had in mind for you in your decision-making. Decisions that involve a man and wife should constitute an amalgamation of both perspectives in order to come to the wisest of decisions.

In summarizing our look at the biblical role of a man in his marriage, I can do no better than to quote the words of Dr Lane Adams: 'I have tried to give up entirely even thinking about whether or not my wife is submissive to me. I've got my hands full trying to determine whether or not I'm truly loving her as Christ loved the church and gave himself for it. Since love never compels, my concern is to evidence a love that constrains.'

The role of the wife

The major function of a woman in marriage is that of submission to her husband's leadership.

> You wives must submit to your husbands' leadership in the same way you submit to the Lord. For a husband is in charge of his wife in the same way Christ is in charge of his body the church. (He gave his very life to take care of it and be its Saviour!) So you wives must willingly obey your husbands in everything, just as the church obeys Christ' (Ephesians 5:22–24 TLB).

I have met a number of women who react negatively to the scriptural teaching of submission. One woman once said to me, 'I've tried this submission business on my husband, but it just doesn't work.' When I asked her what she meant by that statement, she told me how she had for several weeks engaged in actions that were designed to give her husband the impression she was a 'submissive' wife. As she talked, I sensed that there was a 'great gulf fixed' between her actions and her attitudes. Her actions said one thing but her attitudes said another. And so it was no wonder she found the truth of submission a problem.

Another woman said to me, 'I don't mind my husband being the head as long as I can be the neck and turn him whichever way I want him to go!' But ladies, submission is not something to be feared—it is something to be enjoyed. And when rightly understood and practised, it helps a woman experience the security she needs.

The question I am often asked by women, when counselling them with their marital difficulties, is this: what exactly is submission—what does it mean and what does it entail?

Submission is really an attitude or a frame of mind. It recognizes that just as Christ was subject to God, and that the church is subject to Christ, so a woman ought to be subject to her husband. By this attitude she is saying, 'I believe God has arranged the structure of marriage in harmony with the highest principles of the universe. And one of those principles is submission to a higher authority. God has placed my husband above me, not to be superior to me, but to be my spiritual covering and protection. God will protect me from harm *through him*, and as I recognize this principle and live happily and contentedly beneath it, I shall be relieved of a great deal of the stresses and strains of life because God has arranged and equipped my husband to carry them.'

You see, as a wife responds to her husband's leadership, and submits to it, she enjoys protection and fulfilment in the position God designed her to enjoy. Through this divine order, God is able to reach deep into the life of a woman and provide her with the fulfilment she needs.

How to submit to your husband

It is one thing to believe in the scriptural principle of submission—it is another to carry it into one's daily life and practice. How then should a woman go about the duty of submitting herself to her husband?

Firstly, she should transfer to him the responsibility for final decisions. As we saw earlier a wife is designed by God to see things in a perspective which sometimes eludes a man, and this means a wife has an obligation to provide her husband with the benefits of this perspective, but having done so, she should then leave the final decision to him. If after sharing your view of things you feel your husband is making a wrong decision, tell him so, and if he disagrees allow him the privilege to implement that decision the way he sees fit.

Whatever you do, don't nag him about it, and if you feel a serious mistake is about to be made, then take your case to a higher court—talk to God about it. Darien Cooper, a wife who claims that she discovered the key to marital success by learning the principles of submission, gives some helpful advice on this subject. She says,

> A man will value your advice more highly if you are a loving, submissive wife. When he asks your opinion, answer him objectively, sticking to the issues and the facts involved. Remember, men tend to use speech to express ideas and communicate factual information, while women have a tendency to use speech to express feelings or vent their emotions. As you give your opinion, try not to lead with your emotions, but briefly share, on the basis of the facts, your thoughts concerning the situation.

But what should a woman do if she feels her husband needs her opinion and he doesn't ask for it? She should give it nevertheless, but in the spirit of Proverbs 31:26, 'She opens her mouth with skillful and godly Wisdom and in her tongue is the law of kindness—giving counsel and instruction' (AMP.). If you ask yourself: how will my words affect my husband; will it make him feel inferior or jeopardize his role as the leader?—then you will be more apt to obey what the writer of Proverbs was talking about, the law of kindness.

Secondly, give your husband all the respect you can muster. A man thrives in his role as a spiritual leader when he is assured of the respect of his wife. In a seminar where the principles of submission were being shared with a number of women, someone said, 'God has given you the power to turn your man into the man both you and God want him to be—that power is the power of respect.'

One woman, hearing this, decided there and then she would seek to develop within herself a greater respect for her husband who was not a Christian. She went home and watched him carefully in everything he did at the same time praying, 'Lord, help me to be alert to the abilities and qualities of my husband so that I can genuinely offer him my respect.'

Gradually it began to dawn on her that her husband had qualities which she knew were there, but she had never really pinpointed to herself. The first thing that struck her was the way he disciplined the children, firmly but lovingly. Then she noticed the way in which he always kept his word, not only to her but to other people as well. After a few weeks of noting these qualities, she began to share with her husband the growing feelings of respect she had for him. She complimented him on such things as his intellectual ability, his honesty, the way in which he disciplined the children and so on. She took advantage of every opportunity to communicate, both verbally and non-verbally, the respect she felt for her husband, and after a few months, she noticed that her husband had changed out of all proportion. He was more considerate of her Christian commitment, more tolerant of her church-going, and one day asked if he might accompany her to church.

The minister of the church preached that day, I am told, one of the greatest evangelistic messages of his career, which resulted in the man surrendering his life to Jesus Christ. When later he himself attended a seminar on the subject of marital relationships and heard the speaker tell the women about the importance of respecting their husbands, he raised his hand and asked if he might contribute a personal testimony on that point. He was permitted to do so, and this is what he said: 'When my wife began to show me respect, although I didn't realize what was happening, it created for me a bigger mould into which I wanted to pour myself. I wanted so much to be the man she saw me to be. And it was this that led eventually to my desire to receive Christ.'

In Ephesians 5:33 Paul says, 'Let the wife see that she respects and reverences her husband—that she notices him, regards him, honours him, prefers him, venerates and esteems him; and that she defers to him, praises him, and loves and admires him exceedingly' (AMP.). Nothing will be too big for your husband to achieve if he has your support, your admiration and your respect.

Thirdly, be wise in the way you handle money. Inability to handle money is one of the commonest causes of irritation between a husband and wife. A man likes to feel that his wife is responsible in the way she manages the finances of the home. The Bible speaks about a happy man as one who is able to trust his wife in the area of buying and selling, so it is quite scriptural for a man to commit money matters to his wife if she is wise in that area. Listen to what the writer of the book of Proverbs says about such a wife: 'Her husband can trust her, and she will richly satisfy his needs.... She goes out to inspect a field, and buys it; with her own hands she plants a vineyard.... She makes belted linen garments to sell to the merchants' (Proverbs 31:11, 16, 24, TLB).

When money is in short supply, a wife's attitude towards the problem and her husband's efforts to bring in the money can either make or break him. Men feel as if they are failures when they have difficulty in providing the family budget. Some who do not have the loving support of their wives have turned to alcohol, or to other women, and even to suicide in times of financial crisis. If you scold, pout or nag your husband because of difficulties he might be experiencing in bringing in the family income, you could push him over the edge into physical or even mental sickness.

You can greatly assist in times of financial crisis by resisting those special 'bargains' and curtailing the desire to purchase that 'perfect' dress at a greatly reduced price. Be careful also that a desire for 'things' does not kill your husband's incentive at work. Develop confidence in God's ability to assist you with your finances, and put your trust in him rather than in material things. God warns us against trying to gain security from material things: 'He who leans on, trusts and is confident in his riches shall fall, but the (uncompromisingly) righteous shall flourish like a green bough' (Proverbs 11:28 AMP.).

Fourthly, ask God to show you any areas in which you may have assumed leadership. If you have deliberately, or unconsciously, assumed the role of leadership in your home, then begin at once to reverse the situation by *gradually* transferring to your husband the responsibilities he finds it most easy to accept.

Elinor, a woman in her mid-forties, came to a seminar where I was teaching on the subject of marriage relationships. During the session on marital roles, she came to the conclusion that she had assumed the role of leadership, and decided there and then that when she returned home, she would share this fact with her husband. She arrived home that evening to find her husband sitting in a chair watching his favourite sports programme on television. Without a word she went upstairs, collected all the domestic accounts which she normally paid, together with the cheque book, then came downstairs, dumped the lot in his lap and said, 'You are the leader—so lead.'

Well, you just can't do that to a man who is in the

middle of watching his favourite sports programme and get away with it! The man, of course, exploded in anger and asked her what she meant. 'I've been to a seminar today,' she said, 'at which I saw that we had been living in reversed roles. Because of your weakness as a leader, I have had to do the things you should have been doing. But I'm not doing it any more—from now on you are the leader, and you can start by taking over the accounts and paying all the bills.' This was too much for the man to take, and, without a word, he left the house and wasn't heard of for three days. When the shock of his wife's action had finally worn off, he returned to confess that he had not taken his place as the leader in his home, and that from then on things would be different.

I would not recommend this type of approach myself, although in Elinor and Bill's situation it seemed to work! A better way is gradual transfer of responsibilities. You can begin by telling the children to 'go and ask Daddy: he's the head of our home' whenever they seek a major decision. It may be as much of a shock to them as it might be to their father, but it's a good way to start. The best way to encourage your husband as a leader is to be a good follower. Tell him how much you enjoy him taking charge of things. It may be difficult at first, but as you ease yourself out of the leadership role a little at a time, making sure you compliment your husband every time he discharges his responsibility, he will soon become enthusiastic about being the head of the house.

Fifthly, determine to obey God's word irrespective of whether you feel like it or not. If you find the biblical principle of submission difficult to come to terms with, then confess this to the Lord and talk to him about it. I have discovered through counselling hundreds of women over the past thirty years that if a woman finds it difficult to submit to her husband the problem is much deeper than that—she really finds it difficult to submit to the Lord. In joyfully submitting to her husband, a woman is saying, 'Lord, I trust you in everything and if this is your commandment to me then I willingly obey it, knowing it is for my ultimate benefit and my happiness.' If you find it difficult to submit yourself to your husband, it could be that deep-down you are having difficulty in totally trusting the Lord. Perhaps you feel that if you don't stand up for yourself, and be assertive, then things won't work out the way they ought.

Pause for a moment and think this through with me. Have you ever had a problem with the commandment, 'You shall not steal'? Probably not. You accepted it as a command of God, and came to the conclusion that God undoubtedly never intended us to steal. You believe it, abide by it, because God has commanded it. Now the same thing applies to submission. I didn't say, 'God said it,' but, 'God *commanded* it.' So accept it as a commandment of God, and decide to abide by it irrespective of how you feel.

Next, consider the fact that God, in placing your husband in the position of headship, has your interests as well as your husband's in mind. He wants you to feel secure, relaxed and free from strain. 'But how can I be relaxed and free from strain,' you say, 'when I have doubts about my husband's ability to lead? I know I can do a better job myself.' Well, this is where your willingness to trust God comes in. As you commit yourself to doing what God asks, and concentrate on maintaining as willing an attitude as you can, God will be able to deal with your husband directly, and will not be hindered by a rebellious or resistant wife. It is utterly amazing the changes God can make in a man when his wife stays in the place where God wants her to be. So let go. Relax! You can enjoy the freedom of knowing that as you submit yourself to your husband, God is in final control. He will not allow any harm to come to you.

As you learn to trust Christ, and give yourself in obedience to his commands, you can experience peace and security even though you don't get the things you want. Your joy doesn't depend on circumstances—or whether or not your husband sees the importance of being a spiritual leader—it depends on your fellowship and obedience to God.

3

COMMUNICATION IS THE KEY

Many marriage counsellors are convinced that one of the greatest obstacles to a successful marriage is an inability to communicate. Ruel Howe in his book *Herein is Love* says: 'If there is any indispensable insight with which a young couple should begin their life together, it is that they should try to keep open, at all costs, the lines of communication between them.'

The importance and value of communication in marriage has added meaning for me as I write this chapter, because having spent a few days preparing my notes on what I am going to say about this issue, I failed to attend to a matter of urgent domestic importance. Naturally my wife became concerned about my failure to attend to the issue, and this morning, in a gentle and loving way, she told me so. The two-hour discussion we had in which we both expressed our feelings on the issue, openly and freely, not only resolved the matter but brought us closer together. As we talked the matter through, using the principles of communication I am going to share with you now, we truly became 'of one mind'. In the early days of our marriage, a discussion like this would have driven us apart. Now, however, using the right principles, it serves to draw us closer to each other. So I'm starting at my desk two hours late this morning. But, believe me, I feel great!

The communication process in marriage consists of three very simple but powerful rules: *talking, listening,* and *understanding.* If you learn these rules and apply them in your marriage then the chances are you will end up being as happy on your ruby wedding anniversary as on the day you were first wed.

Talking

Let's consider the first principle in good communication —talking. Talking is not just the opposite of silence. And talking for the sake of talking is not good communication either. Someone said, 'There are as many perpetual talkers in divorce courts as there are silent couples.' Some talk too much, some talk too little and many talk with little or no meaning. Talking *with point and purpose* is an essential ingredient of effective communication.

A counsellor tells the story of how he was called in to help save a broken marriage. The husband said, 'I can't stand it any more. My wife just talks and talks.' 'What does she talk about?' asked the counsellor. 'Ah, that's the trouble,' said the husband, 'she doesn't say.'

Hugo Bourdeau, a marriage guidance counsellor based in Baltimore, USA, says that the inability to talk with point and purpose shows up in eighty-five out of every hundred couples visiting marriage counsellors. He points out that during courtship, couples spend hours together, sharing attitudes and planning for the future, but after they are married and have set up home, 'the wife's easy conversation often freezes into a mystifying silence and the husband's tender murmurings of courtship days develop into the full lung power of near raving.' A happy marriage is not possible without communication which reveals with reasonable certainty how the other feels about a given action or situation.

Bob came into my church office when I was a minister in

the north of England, slumped into a chair, and said he wanted to divorce his wife. Bob was a successful business-man with a fine house and a grown-up family. 'Since the children have left home,' he said, 'our marriage seems to be over. We never fight, but then we never talk. And the silence is almost driving me crazy.' When I talked to his wife Eileen about it, she said, 'There's nothing to talk about. Whenever we have visited friends in the past he has criticized me for the way I have spoken to them or the things I have said. So I just gave up talking.'

These two people, intelligent and fine-looking, were like two girls I heard about playing a musical duet; when they sensed discord, instead of working it out, they pulled apart and gave up their interest in music. Bob and Eileen's marriage had ground to a halt because they had allowed themselves to become isolated from each other by an invisible but real barrier of resentment.

The first thing I felt it necessary to challenge them on was their resentment, and I encouraged them to forgive each other and start a clean sheet in their marriage. This done, they then agreed to talk out their difficulties, and work on mutually agreed solutions rather than turning away from each other when discord intruded.

A judge who presided over thousands of cases of marriage failure said that his experience in the divorce courts led him to the conclusion that 'bottled-up resent-ments constitute one of the greatest dangers to marriage'. And his advice for overcoming that problem was this—*talk it out*. He said that frank talk will do nothing but good even though the initial response may be shock and wounded pride. I would add two more words of advice, as I believe that for a Christian couple simply to talk it out is insufficient. My advice would rather be: talk it out—in love. Isn't this what the Scripture encourages us to do? Listen to Paul's advice as recorded in Ephesians 4:15, 'Speak the truth in love.' This biblical injunction sums up all the aspects of communication which we are considering and focuses them into five words.

Let's take a closer look at this biblical imperative.

Speak...

This means being willing and ready to talk things out, rather than withdrawing into silence. I am not just thinking here of handling arguments, which is the subject of our next chapter, but rather the need to be open and honest in all things. 'Bill and I don't talk enough,' one wife told me. 'Sometimes I feel we are involved in a guessing game in which I have to think what he is thinking yet I am not allowed to tell him my conclusions. I need him to lead in communication, because if I do, it looks and sounds as if I am a nagging wife.'

This remark led me to ask, 'Why is communication important to you?'

'I need to be talked to,' she replied, 'because when my husband talks to me, somehow it makes me feel more of a person. I feel I am worth something to him when he talks to me, and that he loves me enough to share with me. When he is preoccupied and lapses into periods of silence, I feel I am being pushed out of his world.'

I used to be like Bill, I must confess. When my wife was longing for good, loving conversation, I found silence more consoling. I've had to learn to put her interests first, and when I have done this the rewards have been well worth the effort. In a way that I cannot explain, whenever I have stepped out of myself to give to my wife in conversation, it seems the sharing opens doors in my being through which refreshing bursts of energy pass, bringing both physical and spiritual rejuvenation. A psychiatrist with whom I shared this point said the rejuvenation came from an inner happiness at knowing I was doing God's will by taking steps to make my marriage work.

A marriage counsellor tells of a couple who came for

counselling. 'We have never had an argument in the whole of our marriage,' said the husband. 'How did you accomplish that?' asked the counsellor. The wife replied, 'We just don't talk.'

The key to initiating good conversation is simple: ask questions. Questions are to a good marriage relationship what food is to living. But give some thought to the type of questions you use. When training counsellors to ask the right questions of counsellees, I refer to what is known in counselling circles as low-structure questions and high-structure questions.

A high-structure question is used when a person is nervous or apprehensive and does not require a good deal of thought. For example, 'Where were you born?' or 'What school did you attend?' The answers to these questions require little thought and do not make the counsellee feel threatened in any way.

Low-structure questions are used when the counsellee is a little more relaxed and is in a position to give more thought and attention to the answers. For example, a low-structure question would be, 'What were your feelings when your husband told you he wanted a divorce?' This demands more than a one-word answer and encourages the counsellee to open himself or herself in a deeper way.

With just a little practice you'll soon get the hang of asking questions that stimulate conversation. 'How are you feeling?' might be a good question to ask your partner, but it inevitably evokes no more than a one-word answer such as 'fine' or 'lousy'. The principle of stimulating conversation through questions is to ask questions that encourage the other person to tell you how he or she *feels* about a topic, event, idea, and so on.

Here are some questions taken from a *Marriage Enrichment Seminar* programme which should help you to get the point:

How do you think our marriage has enriched our lives?

What are some of the things we have learned since we have been married?

Are there ways that, in your opinion, I ought to adopt in order to become a better husband/wife?

Is there anything about which you find it difficult to communicate?

Do you feel I accept you as you are—or do you feel a pressure from me to change you?

Do you feel threatened when we disagree about something or I make a decision you don't like?

Do I have habits or mannerisms that offend you?

Is there anything I have done in the past that has caused some resentment to build up in you?

Is there anything in our marriage that is contrary to what the Bible teaches?

Do you feel I fulfill your sexual needs?

Do our children know how much we love them? Do we get it across?

What's the best thing that happened to you today?

Before you begin to put these suggestions into practice pay attention to the following guidelines:

1. **Don't force things.** There will be occasions when neither you nor your partner will feel like discussing anything too deep or too involved. Conversation must flow naturally—sitting together on the couch, out driving in the car, taking a walk, etc.

2. **Look at your partner frequently** when he or she speaks to you. It's not always necessary to look continually at a person when you speak, but it is when they are speaking to you. Except, of course, when you are driving a car!

3. **Keep at it.** You will find at first that some questions just grind to a halt. Your partner might say in response to an open-ended question, 'I don't know,' or 'I don't have an opinion on that matter.' Don't be put off. Pursue the

matter, gently, of course, by saying something like, 'Well, let's think out loud about it together.'

Many married couples I have counselled tell me that these suggestions for developing conversation have brought amazing results in deepening their relationship. Try them for yourself and I'll be surprised if you don't find yourselves growing closer as a result of taking time to talk together.

Before you persecuted men feel too self-righteous, I would like to add that I feel great sympathy for some wives because their husbands rarely talk to them. They never share themselves, talk about their work, or say a word of appreciation or love. I can't begin to count the number of times women have said to me, 'My husband doesn't talk to me.' When I enquire as to what they mean, they tell me that although their husbands use words, there is no real communication. They only communicate with them on a mundane level such as, 'How are you today?' or 'Will you take my suit to the cleaners?' There is no deep and meaningful communication.

John Powell in his book *Why Am I Afraid To Tell You Who I Am?* says that there are five levels of communication in marriage.

Level one: cliché conversation. This is where a person hides behind the safety screen of clichés. There is no personal sharing. Clichés are used, such as, 'How are you today?' or 'Looks like it's going to rain.'

Level two: reporting facts about others. In this kind of conversation people tell others what others have said to them but offer no personal views on those facts. They report facts just like the newsreader.

Level three: ideas and judgements. This, says Powell, is where some real communication begins. The person is willing to step out from behind his safety screen and risk telling someone else of his ideas and judgements.

Level four: feelings and emotions. Here the person

begins to share his feelings about issues. There can be no truly effective communication in marriage until both partners interact with each other on this level. You won't really know your partner until you know how he or she *feels* on vital issues.

Level five: openness and honesty. This is the ultimate level where the relationship is one of absolute openness and honesty. All deep relationships, especially a marriage relationship, must be based on honest communication. If there is no openness and honesty, then the marriage will suffer.

...the truth...

If there is to be good communication between a husband and wife then there must be a commitment to speak the truth in all things—to tell it like it is. Either partner should have the right also to talk about any concern and expect a listening and understanding ear. For ten years of marriage, Michael, a friend of mine, had been living behind a façade of graciousness and charm. Then, after attending a seminar where he heard me talk about the need for openness and honesty in the marriage relationship, he went home and unburdened himself to his wife. He told her of his deep insecurity, his pride, his lust, his desire for approval and his inner fears. His wife was somewhat taken aback by his honesty, for she had no idea of the conflicts that lay beneath her husband's calm and seemingly self-assured exterior. She told me that after the initial shock had worn off, the openness and honesty he displayed allowed her to enter an area of her husband's life from which hitherto she had been excluded.

'Looking back,' she said, 'I can see now that there were times when I felt there was something wrong with our relationship but I couldn't put my finger on it. From the moment he shared with me his fears and anxieties, our marriage, although fairly happy before, moved on to another plane. Now I really feel I "know" him and there has been a sudden sense of the reality of God's presence in our relationship that is unbelievable.' Because the husband had allowed his wife to enter into the depths of his heart he was set free from living behind a mask of pretence. They reached the pinnacle of the ladder we talked about earlier and were now communicating on level five—the level of openness and honesty.

Sometimes a husband and wife are prevented from sharing themselves openly and honestly with their partner for fear that if they do, they might hurt their partner's feelings. This more often than not is a cop-out. Speaking the truth may hurt and then again it may not. But that is not the point. Communication can only be developed along the lines of truth, and whatever hurts may come, then these have to be faced, for open and honest communication is worth all the hassles that are involved. 'When you consider lying to avoid unpleasantness,' says one Christian counsellor, 'you should be brutally honest with yourself about your inner motivation. Are you really afraid of hurting your partner? Or is it yourself you are worried about? Are you just trying to ease out of an unpleasant situation because you think it isn't worth the hassle?'

I am often asked the question, 'But aren't there times in a marriage when it is more loving to lie? Isn't it better to lie, just a little, to avoid unpleasantness?' My response to that question is this: lying may avoid unpleasantness for a while, but in the long run it causes even more unpleasantness. It sours the soul of the one who hides the truth and, remember, lies, even 'little' ones, have a way of being discovered, and when they are found out, there is even more hurt and unpleasantness.

... *in love*

In cultivating openness and honesty in the marriage

relationship, truth must always be expressed in love. Honest sharing does not mean tearing someone apart verbally. Some people think that being honest and speaking the truth are all that is required to maintain good communication lines in marriage, but it isn't—truth must be shared in love. In fact, you don't have the right to share the truth in your marriage unless you do it in love.

Truth without love rips and tears, and leaves a person feeling grieved and desolated. Truth with love sometimes also hurts but, like the Africans say when an antiseptic is put on a cut, 'It hurts good.' No one has the right to be obnoxious and abusive in sharing the truth. Glaring, name-calling, blaming, accusations and sarcasm are unscriptural ways of sharing the truth.

In the early part of my ministry, I pastored a church where one of the elders was renowned for his honesty and ability to tell it like it is! His problem, however, was that he could never share the truth in a spirit of love. On several occasions I heard him say to certain members of the church whom he thought needed reprimanding, 'Now, I'm telling you in love. . . .' But one had only to look at his angry countenance and the red veins standing out on his neck to know that whatever the truth he was uttering was being cancelled out in the minds and hearts of the hearers by the manner and attitude in which he said it. I spoke to him many times about the matter, but he used to reply: 'That is the way I am and I'm too old to change now.' I warned him that if he didn't change, he would not only damage the lives of others but would damage himself physically and spiritually.

Some years later, after I had left that church, I heard a report from one of the church officers that in a heated argument in a deacon's meeting, just seconds after he uttered the words, 'Now, I'm telling you in love, brother. . .' he slumped across the table—dead. A member of his family told me, when I wrote expressing my condolences, that the family doctor had said, 'His anger killed him.' Despite his problem many people, of course, loved him, but I know a number, too, who were so desolated after an encounter with him that they turned away altogether from the faith. I say again, no one has the right to share truth unless they share it in love.

Speaking the truth in love means a commitment to using only appropriate words. The Bible speaks a good deal about the power of our words. Proverbs 18:21 states, 'Death and life are in the power of the tongue' (NASB). Proverbs 26:22 speaks of how words really get to a person: 'The words of a whisperer...go down into the innermost parts of the body' (NASB). James 3:2–10 talks about the power of words and why it is so important to control the tongue. When God spoke in Genesis 1:2, he created a world—a world of beauty and harmony. When you speak, you, too, create a world—a world of beauty or a world of misery.

According to Scripture, a husband or wife who blurts out things without considering the feelings of their partner is in a bad way spiritually. 'Do you see a man who is hasty in his words? There is more hope for a fool than for him' (Proverbs 29:20, NASB). The apostle Peter sums it up beautifully when he says, 'If you want a happy, good life, keep control of your tongue, and guard your lips' (1 Peter 3:10 TLB). This commitment to using only appropriate words means that words that are harsh-sounding like 'dummy', 'stupid', 'fathead', etc., are out. 'A word fitly spoken is like apples of gold in pictures of silver' (Proverbs 25:11). Concentrate on choosing words that carry a positive and helpful message.

Speaking the truth in love means supplementing the right use of words with the right tone of voice. Communication experts say that the words we use play a lesser role in the communication process than the tone of voice. The words we use, they tell us, compose just 7% of a message;

the tone of voice, 38%; and non-verbal communication (expression on our face, the look in our eyes, etc.), 55%. Take, for example, the words, 'I love you.' These are beautiful and meaningful words. But the words by themselves convey only 7% of a message, and unless they are complemented by the right tone of voice they can lose much of their intrinsic meaning. It is possible to say, 'I love you,' in a dull, flat monotone voice that almost contradicts the meaning of the words. So, remember, it is not always what you say that is important, but the tone of voice in which you say it.

Speaking the truth in love means using truth as observation and not as accusation. Your partner is likely to be less defensive if you speak the truth in a manner that shows you are accepting responsibility for your own feelings about the issue. Let me explain. If you say to your partner, 'You are careless and sloppy about the house,' this is accusatory and your partner will become defensive. But if you communicate what you are feeling by prefacing it with the words, 'I am,' or 'I feel,' then you have expressed the feeling with ownership—as something inside of you—rather than being accusatory. It would be better, then, to say, 'I feel upset when the house is untidy.' This helps your partner to understand that you are being honest about your feelings, yet being careful not to be condemning or accusing.

Listening

Having looked more closely at what it is to speak the truth in love, let's consider now the second principle in good communication. The experts in communication tell us that *listening* is something that does not come naturally to us; it is not our natural preference. Most people prefer to be talkers rather than listeners. We are more inclined—especially when we feel hurt or angry—to assert our opinion and express our feelings. Because of this, we focus more on getting our words into a conversation rather than giving our full attention to what the other person is saying.

'The trouble with you is you don't listen to me,' said Joyce to her husband Brian, during a counselling session in which I was involved. 'And the trouble with you,' said Brian, 'is you don't understand a word I say.' It took several weeks for Joyce and Brian to learn the three basic principles of communication, but those weeks of concentration and practice gave them, as they put it, 'a key that opened all the locked doors in our relationship.'

An anonymous author presented the value of listening thus:

> Listen...
> Do you care to know my deep feeling within?
> The struggle...the pain?
> Will you share my joy,
> And help to validate my soul?
> Then listen.
> If you will hear, I will tell the truth,
> If you can understand, I will open the secret vault,
> And we will draw near to each other
> And both be blessed.

The Bible gives us some good advice on the importance of listening. Proverbs 18:13 says, 'What a shame—yes, how stupid!—to decide before knowing the facts!' (TLB). James 1:19 in the Amplified Bible reads, 'Let every man be quick to hear, (a ready listener,) slow to speak, slow to take offense and to get angry.'

According to the Scripture, listening means making an effort to concentrate on what a person is saying, and being as eager to listen as you are to speak. Someone wittily suggested that the reason why God made us with one mouth but two ears is because he wanted us to listen twice as much as we speak! Some communication experts have recently coined a term to describe poor listening habits. It is called 'egospeak'. Egospeak is defined in several ways. One definition is: 'Thinking about what you are going to say once the other person has stopped talking.' Another is: 'Jumping in before the other person has finished their part of the conversation.' Watch carefully and you will probably spot 'egospeak' in almost every conversation you hear. No wonder listeners have become an endangered species.

Good listening is something that has to be learned. The trouble is that, whilst most of us have been taught to express ourselves with the right use of words, we have never been taught to listen. How then do we go about learning to listen?

First, we must recognize the obstacles that prevent us from effective listening, and work on removing them. One of the first obstacles is defensiveness. This was pin-pointed in a recent counselling session with Alice, who told me that she was having a communication problem in her marriage. 'When are you a poor listener?' I asked her. After thinking the question through for a few minutes, she said, 'When I am on the defensive. Yesterday Bert, my husband, mentioned a problem we have not yet resolved and I could feel all my barriers go up. I began to think up all the reasons why he was wrong and I was right. I realize now that, because I was focusing on what I was feeling, I was not really listening to what he was saying.'

Actually defensiveness is a common problem in family arguments. Paul Tournier, the famous Swiss medical doctor and counsellor, says, 'How beautiful, how grand and liberating this experience when people learn to listen to each other. It is impossible to overemphasize the immense need people have to be listened to. Listen to all the conversations of our world, those between nations as well as those between couples. They are, for the most part, *dialogues of the deaf*' (italics mine). Someone has described most dialogues that go on in marriage as 'duelogues', in which each person is busy thinking up ways in which they can shoot down the other person's comments. I know I need to work more on my own defensiveness when it comes to this matter of listening. Do you?

Another obstacle to effective listening is self-centredness or self-preoccupation. Jim, a burly six-foot-four army sergeant, once responded to my question in a counselling session, 'Why are you a poor listener?' in this way: 'I think it's an ego need I have—a need to talk rather than to listen. I get more satisfaction from talking than from listening. That I know for sure. I butt in to my wife's conversations without waiting for her to finish. Then it ends up with her not wanting to finish what she was saying.' Jim came to recognize that his tendency to interrupt his wife, and not hear her out, stemmed from the fact that he was more interested in himself than he was in her. As he focused on developing genuine love (something we will be dealing with in a later chapter) he became a better listener.

Yet another obstacle to good listening is physical or mental fatigue. Carol, a middle-aged housewife with marital problems, said, 'My husband and I have been seeing that troubles arise when we try to discuss important issues at the wrong time. There are times when, quite honestly, I am *too tired* to listen well. Physical fatigue, something I experience at the end of almost every day, makes listening a great burden.' I suggested that the remedy, quite simply, was to talk about serious and important issues only when she was rested and alert. Mental and physical fatigue dulls our ability to listen. Make sure before you embark upon serious conversation that you are not tired.

These three obstacles to good listening are not the only

ones to cause problems in the communication process, but they are among the major ones. Learn to identify the obstacles to listening in your own relationship and start taking some practical steps to overcome them.

Secondly, in order to become a good listener, we must learn not simply to listen to a person's words but to the feelings which lie beneath those words. Jesse Nirenberg in her book *Getting Through To People* said:

> Conversation is the main vehicle for expressing feelings as well as ideas. And since feelings are continually looking for outlets, we can see that conversations are bound to be filled with feelings, some erupting and others edging their way out.

There is no better way of assuring a person that you are a perceptive listener than when you identify the feeling that lies underneath the words. To spotlight the feeling and label it is the quickest way to making a person feel understood. And when a person feels understood, he or she becomes less defensive and more co-operative.

Take Philip and Rita, for example. In a counselling session I had with them, Rita said, 'What's the use of trying to make a go of it with Philip? Nothing I do seems to help. I try my hardest to do things to please him but it's all to no avail.' I turned to Philip and said, 'How would you describe your wife's feelings at this moment?' He replied, 'I think she is sorry for herself.' Notice his words carefully —'I think....' I asked him to describe his wife's feelings, but he responded by giving me a rational evaluation of her behaviour. No wonder she didn't feel understood.

My response, looking in from the outside, was different from his. I said, 'I'm hearing Rita say she is feeling a sense of hopelessness. She has tried again and again but feels trapped by failure.' Then turning to Rita, I said, 'Is that what you are feeling?' She immediately burst into tears, and after sobbing her heart out for several minutes, she said, 'You put your finger right on the spot; *hopeless* is exactly how I feel.'

Later in that counselling session, I felt it necessary to speak rather pointedly to Rita about her unsubmissive behaviour, to which she responded, 'I have never permitted anyone, not even my minister, to mention the word submission to me before, but I felt that you understood me better than anyone I have ever known, so I determined in my heart that I would listen to you without resistance.' Can you see what had happened? Because on this occasion I had accurately pinpointed her feelings (honesty compels me to admit I am not always that accurate), Rita felt that I understood her problem, and thus became less defensive when it came to the challenge I presented to her from the Scriptures.

Philip was greatly intrigued by what went on in that counselling session and said, 'Whenever anyone mentioned the word submission to my wife, she would hit the roof. I can't believe what I am seeing here today.' He realized that to pinpoint a person's feelings enables them to feel greatly understood, and as he began to practise this in his marriage, his relationship with Rita improved tremendously. I know of no other area of communication which has been more rewarding for me as a husband or counsellor than listening to the feelings that lie beneath words. I still have to discipline myself to practise this skill—especially in family relationships—but the more I do it, the greater the results.

Listening for feelings is not an easy skill to master. Therefore, as an exercise, I have listed below a number of feeling statements for you to analyse. Imagine these statements being made by your husband or wife, and fill in what you consider is the appropriate feeling response.

'Shouldn't you stay at home tonight? I've been on my own every night this week.'
Feeling . . . . . .
'When I ask a question, you never seem to give me a clear and easily understood answer.'
Feeling . . . . . .
'It seems all I do in this house is go around picking up clothes that have not been put back in their proper place. If this doesn't stop, I'll go mad.'
Feeling . . . . . .
'I made this all by myself. I think it's pretty.'
Feeling . . . . . .
'I work hard to bring the money home, and when you spend it on unnecessary items I get upset.'
Feeling . . . . . .

Consider the following list of emotions which might help you pinpoint the true feeling behind the above statements.

Hurt	Inferiority	Disappointment
Humiliation	Rejection	Impatience
Loneliness	Jealousy	Superiority
Intimidation	Sympathy	Trapped
Anger	Acceptance	Unloved
Happiness	Sadness	Confidence
Frustration	Hopelessness	Shyness
Shame	Pleasure	Despair

Without practice and intense listening, few people can distinguish the above emotions in a conversation. Practise the skill of differentiating emotions, and begin to use it as and when appropriate.

Let me mention one more point that might help you in the development of the skill of perceptive listening—repeat to the other person precisely what you have heard them say. Most of us have seen that little motto that frequently appears on cards and posters: 'I know you believe you understand what you think I said, but I am not sure you realize that what you have heard is not what I meant.' It makes a point, doesn't it?

Communication between one person and another—sender and receiver—is often distorted without one or both persons knowing it. When we restate to another person what we have heard them say, we give them the chance to confirm or deny the accuracy of what we have understood them to say. Here's an example of what I have in mind.

Wife: I really get upset with these newspapers and magazines all over the place. They are in the bedroom, the living room, the kitchen. I wish you would be more thoughtful.

Husband: Just so I don't misunderstand what you are saying, let me reflect what I hear you saying. You are upset because I leave newspapers all over the house without putting them in one place, and you see that as not being considerate of your needs. Is that right?

Wife: Yes.

Husband: Then I'm deeply sorry and in future I will do my utmost to consider you, and put the newspapers and magazines in one place.

Now naturally one should not carry this principle too far and employ it in every conversation. That would be ridiculous and would prove counter-productive. But in any conversation where what is heard is important and crucial to the building of good relationships, then this is a practice that ought to be employed. There are many reasons why reflecting to a person what he or she has said is important. First, it is so easy for a listener to *misinterpret* what another person has said. Just recently I was teaching in a Counselling Seminar, and I turned to one of the students and said, 'Do you know what I mean?' 'Yes,' he said. 'I know exactly what you mean.' 'Then please reflect to me what you think I mean.' He did, and he was a million miles off the mark. In fact, what he had heard was exactly the opposite of what I had said.

Ever played the game 'Rumour'? This is where one person whispers a message to the person next to him, who whispers it to a third person, and so on around the room until the message returns to the one who started the game. The distortion that usually occurs is often quite humorous.

A story is told how during the First World War, when communication systems were not as they are today, a message was passed down by the men in the trenches to a runner whose task it was to convey it to the officers behind the lines. The message started off, 'We are going to advance—send reinforcements.' When it got to the end of the line, it was, 'We are going to a dance—send three and fourpence.'

Restating a message to the other person's satisfaction is seldom done by married couples. A husband rarely says, 'I want to be certain I understand you correctly—let me tell you what I think I heard you say.' More likely he assumes that what he thought he heard was what his wife meant. But this is not always so. Faulty listening skills and his own internal filters could have changed the message.

One author points out that restating a message to the other person's satisfaction shows not only a desire for accurate communication but demonstrates a commitment to your partner's well-being. You are letting him or her know that you are interested in, and care about, what he or she feels. Reflecting to your partner on appropriate occasions what he or she has said can contribute to good feelings and relationships. So learn to listen. It can bring about a transformation in your marriage.

Understanding

Let's consider now the third and final component of the

communication process—understanding. If every husband and wife spent as much time trying to understand their partner as they do in seeking to be understood, there would be fewer hassles and problems in the marriage. Paul Tournier, writing on the matter of understanding one's partner in marriage, said:

> You know well the beautiful prayer of Francis of Assisi: 'Lord, grant that I may seek more to understand than be understood....' As long as a man is pre-occupied primarily with being understood by his wife, he is miserable, overcome with self-pity, the spirit of demanding and bitter withdrawal. As soon as he becomes pre-occupied with understanding her, seeking to understand that which he had not before understood, and with his own wrongdoing in not having understood her, then the direction taken by events begins to change. As soon as a person feels understood, he opens up, and because he lowers his defences, he is also able to make himself better understood.

Husbands and wives should not only focus on this issue but they ought to become pre-occupied with it—lost in it—engrossed with it. There's an old saying that to understand all is to forgive all, and nowhere is that more true than in marriage. When your wife or husband behaves in ways that cause you some irritation, make a deliberate effort to try to understand what causes them to behave in the way they do. All behaviour is caused, say the psychologists, and they are right. There are reasons why we behave the way we do. The reasons may not be apparent at first, but with a little effort they can be pinpointed. This then brings enlightenment and greater understanding. Everyone's background and environment are different, and we bring this background with us into the marriage relationship.

Jim, a thirty-year-old computer operator, married for just three years, said to me once, 'I just can't understand my wife. Whenever I say something sharply to her, she just falls apart and sobs for hours. Her reactions are so much out of proportion to the event that I find it impossible to live with. I have asked her why she reacts in this way and she doesn't know. I mean, in most marriages people speak sharply to each other at times, but it doesn't bring such dramatic reactions such as my wife exhibits. What can I do?'

'Sounds to me like transference,' I said.

'Transference?' said Jim. 'The only transference I can see is the transference of her silly and foolish feelings onto me.'

'No, that's not what I mean by transference,' I replied. 'Transference is the phenomenon that goes on in a person when they project some problem of the past—a bad relationship, a traumatic event or something like that—onto a person or a situation in the present. Sit down one evening, and in a non-threatening manner, talk the problem over with your wife. Try to find what is causing it, but remember to approach her kindly, lovingly, without projecting blame.'

Jim did as I suggested, and came back to me a week later to report what had transpired. 'It took me a few evenings to get to the bottom of the problem,' he said, 'but we made it with patience and persistence.' It seems that his wife, Beatrice, had been brought up by a father who was extremely harsh and belligerent. Many times when she was a girl she had cried herself to sleep—hurt by her father's sharp and cruel manner. Beatrice, though now an adult, still carried within her the inner child of the past—the child that had been barricaded by sharp words, harsh tones and cruel insults. Unconsciously, she was projecting onto her husband, whenever he used a sharp tone of voice, the feelings she had towards her father, and it was this that caused her to react as she did. Jim went on to say, 'As soon as we both realized this, the enlightenment that came worked as if by magic. Beatrice said, "I'm no longer going to be a slave to my past," and I said, "Now I understand what makes you tick." The result is that we are now closer than ever. And even if Beatrice never overcomes her problem, I now have the key to understanding her, and I know I shall approach the situation with much more tenderness and compassion than I did in the past.'

There is no area in marriage that requires greater understanding than the area of inner motivation—why we say and do the things we do. Wherever I go, whether in seminars, in rallies, in conferences or in private homes, people come up to me and say, 'I just can't understand my wife/husband—the way they behave and the things they say completely baffle me.' A book that I have recommended time and time again to people who have difficulty in understanding their partners—or indeed in understanding themselves—is entitled, *Your Inner Child of the Past* by W. Hugh Missildine, MD (Simon & Schuster, London). His thesis is that you were once a child and that child lives on within you—influencing and interfering in your adult life and relationships. When you learn how to spot the inner child of the past, both in yourself and in others, and deal with it through suggested coping strategies, then you discover a new dimension in personal relationships. 'There are six people in every marriage bed,' says Missildine, 'the husband and wife, the father and mother of the husband and the father and mother of the wife.' One couple to whom I recommended this book said, after perusing it, 'If someone had given us this book prior to marriage, it would have saved fifteen years of problems which almost brought us to the brink of divorce.'

I'm reminded as I write of Joyce and Matthew, a young couple I knew in a church I once pastored. Joyce came to me and complained, 'I just can't understand my husband. He knows I have a degree in English Literature, but

whenever I correct his English, or suggest he has constructed a sentence wrongly, he gets overcome with anger.'
I shared with her the phenomenon of transference, and tentatively suggested, 'You remind him of his mother who, unless I am greatly mistaken, must have been a strong and dominant personality who was always correcting him. Have a chat with Matthew one evening about this, and see what results it brings. But, remember, don't threaten him or attempt to force him into conversation, but try to understand what makes him tick. Be gentle and loving—then come back and let me know how you have got on.'

'It's remarkable,' said Joyce when she next came to see me. 'You hit the nail right on the head. Yes, his mother was dominant and was always correcting him.' I said, 'Don't think you are suddenly going to eradicate his fear of dominant women, but if you unconsciously slip into the role of a corrective mother, he will probably always react in this manner. A lot of repressed anger is still inside him towards his mother, which, when you adopt the corrective mother role, is displaced onto you. Now that you understand this, be patient, be loving—give up the mother role and be a wife.' Joyce did as I suggested, and although it took her a long time to move away from the corrective mother role to that of a wife, she eventually succeeded and their marriage was lifted into a new and higher dimension. When we take the time and trouble to learn what makes our partner tick—what the other one likes or dislikes, *why* they behave and feel the way they do—then we open up lines of communication that cannot fail to be rewarding.

The Scripture, of course, has taught this principle for close on two thousand years. Long ago the apostle Paul taught the Ephesians to develop good, personal relationships and to live in a becoming way 'with complete lowliness of mind (humility) and meekness (unselfishness, gentleness, mildness), with patience, bearing with one another and making allowances because you love one another' (Ephesians 4:2 AMP.).

And Paul had the same thing in mind when he wrote to the Philippians and said, 'Then make me truly happy by loving each other and agreeing wholeheartedly with each other, working together with one heart and one mind and purpose. Don't be selfish; don't live to make a good impression on others. Be humble, thinking of others as better than yourself. Don't just think about your own affairs, but be interested in others, too, and in what they are doing' (Philippians 2:2–4 TLB).

So the next time your partner behaves in ways that seem perplexing and strange, don't say, 'I just can't understand you.' Instead take a leaf out of Francis of Assisi's book and send a prayer to heaven: 'Lord, grant that I may seek more to understand than be understood.' If you make this your honest plea, then providing you have given time and attention to the other components of good communication—talking and listening—you will be well on the way to establishing a communication system that can transform your marriage.

4

HOW TO
'FIGHT' LIKE A CHRISTIAN!

'After five years of marriage,' says J. A. Fritz in his book *The Essence of Marriage,* 'there is no longer any excuse for a quarrel between a husband and wife.' Unrealistic? Well, maybe. But there is no doubt (to my mind, at least) that if a couple determine to establish in the first few years of marriage some clear guidelines for handling conflict they can look forward to enjoying the rest of their lives with a minimum of marital discord.

A few months before my own marriage on April 10th, 1951, some of my married friends thought it necessary to share with me their favourite jokes about husband-wife relationships. 'There are two sides to every argument,' said one, 'and they are usually married to each other.' 'How's your wife?' I innocently asked another friend. 'Oh,' he said, 'she's not speaking to me—and I'm in no mood to interrupt.' 'We've been married fifteen years,' said another, 'and in that time we have had just one argument.' 'Really?' I said somewhat naïvely. 'Yes,' joked my friend, 'it started the day we were married and it has not stopped since.'

During these few months leading up to my marriage, I pondered the thought: is marriage a life of bliss or a constant battleground? I discovered that it was a little of both.

A year or two after I was married I sensed that unless Enid and I established some clear guidelines for handling friction, our marriage would end up on the rocks. At that time there was little written on the subject, so I drew up my own set of rules. These rules have been modified, of course, over the years, but basically they remain unchanged. They have helped me weather a number of storms, and as I have shared them with hundreds of others, they too have found them to be of great help and support. I offer them now to you in the hope that they will help you settle your differences in a biblical and spiritual way.

Recognize that conflict is inevitable

Every marriage has periods of argument, friction and conflict. Even some of the greatest saints in the Bible hit some difficult times in their marriages. Look at Abraham (Genesis 16), Isaac (Genesis 27), Jacob (Genesis 30–31), David (2 Samuel 6) and, of course, Hosea.

Jay Hall, an American research expert, who has looked deeply into the subject of conflict resolution, defines conflict in this way: 'Conflict exists whenever there are important differences between people which, should they persist and remain unsolved, serve to keep them apart in some way.' Somewhat simplistic you may think, but then he adds this important statement: 'Conflict arises because all of us perceive people and situations differently.' Someone put it like this.

> Take a man and a woman
> From totally different homes
> With different upbringing and experiences
> Each with emotional uniqueness
> With different likes and dislikes,
> Each with some degree of independence

And with some self-centredness
Living in the same house
With different tasks and responsibilities
Working from the same household budget
Trying to meet the same goals
Will they agree on everything?
No way.

No matter how mature and loyal the marriage partners, the fact that a husband and wife are two distinct people makes some degree of conflict inevitable. Discord and disagreement *will* take place. But it's all part of growing together. Conflict provides for growth and development in the marital relationship and can, if used rightly, build up rather than tear down family unity. 'Conflict,' says Norman Wright, 'is like dynamite. It can be helpful if used in the right way, but can also be destructive if used at the wrong time or in the wrong manner.' Through conflict a person can share his differences with another individual, spot communication gaps and personal weaknesses and then, as these things are explored together, each can learn from the other. And when the conflict is resolved, the growth that comes about in the lives of the couple involved is incredible. My wife and I have grown as much through our conflicts as through our good times together. So don't side-step the inevitable. Recognize that conflicts will surely come, but determine in your heart to make them a strengthening agent and not a destructive one.

Peace at any price?

James Fairfield, a Christian marriage guidance counsellor, claims that there are five common ways in which couples go about the task of dealing with marital conflicts.

The first is to *withdraw* from conflict by adopting the attitude, 'Well, I can't win, so what's the use?' Another way is to *win at all costs*. This method of coping with conflict says, in effect, relationships are secondary—the important thing is to win an argument. A third way is to *yield*. This means giving in in order to get along. A person reasons, 'I don't like this situation but I'll swallow my own opinions in order to get along.' The fourth way is to *compromise*. A person may think, 'I'll give in to some of my partner's demands in order to achieve some of my own. I don't want either of us to be losers all the time.'

All of these approaches to conflict, says Fairfield, are wrong. The right approach, the fifth one, is a determination to *resolve* the conflict. This attitude reasons thus: conflicts are normal and though the tension and pressure is sometimes difficult to handle, I know it is possible to work through the problems to a mutually acceptable solution.

These five common styles of responding to conflict have been observed and verified in the clinical experiences of many psychiatrists, ministers, psychologists and marriage guidance counsellors. The chances are that you have already adopted one of these styles in dealing with your own family conflicts. The only style a Christian can adopt is that of resolution. *Withdrawing* means losing an opportunity to utilize the conflict for spiritual and psychological growth. *Winning* is not concerned with building good relationships only in satisfying one's own personal need for conquest. *Yielding* may appear on the surface to want to preserve a relationship but it does so at the expense of being open and honest about one's own feelings. *Compromise* tends to lower the standards of both parties in order to achieve peaceful co-existence, and fails to deal with the problem at its roots.

When we are faced with conflict in marriage, we normally respond with one of the styles listed above, and if this doesn't work, we shift to our next preference. The style we select is usually the one our parents used in handling their disagreements. A father who sets out to win every argument will influence his son or daughter to follow that response. As a child you observed and were influenced by your parent's styles of coping with conflict, and unless you became aware of what was happening and broke away from it, the chances are that you copy them and develop a similar style in your own marital relationship.

Take a moment now to identify your usual response to conflict. Think about a specific conflict you may have faced recently. Try to remember the feeling you had about your partner. How did you react? Did you withdraw, win, yield, compromise, or set out to resolve the conflict so that the issue was thoroughly dealt with in every way? Put a tick against the response listed below which you think you mostly follow in your relationship. If it is against any other than the word 'resolve', then determine in your heart that, with God's help, you will move in the future towards resolving all your conflicts in a spirit of truth and grace.

☐ *resolve*

☐ *compromise*

☐ *yield*

☐ *win*

☐ *withdraw*

Focus on learning how to control anger

'Anger,' it has been said, 'is the most troublesome emotion for a Christian to handle and the curse of personal relationships.' It certainly is. The Bible in one place condones anger: 'In your anger do not sin,' and then, in another, condemns it: 'Get rid of all... anger' (Ephesians 4:26 and 31, NIV). Does the Scripture contradict itself? No, for there is a righteous and an unrighteous anger. How do we differentiate between the two?

First, let's lay down a basic definition of anger. The dictionary defines it as *strong displeasure*. Rage and fury are closely related, but fury can be more destructive and rage more justified by circumstances. In the New Testament, there are two main Greek words for anger—*thumos* and *orge*. *Thumos* means turbulent commotion, boiling, agitation of feelings, a sudden explosion of anger, bursting upwards then subsiding, much like a match that flares up quickly and then burns out rapidly (Ephesians 4:31 and Galatians 5:20, etc.). *Orge* has the connotation of a more settled and long-lasting attitude of anger which moves on unrestrained towards the goal of seeking revenge (Ephesians 4:31, Colossians 3:8, Matthew 5:22, James 1:20, etc.). *Orge* can be likened to 'coals slowly warming up to red then white hot and holding the high temperature until they cool again'.

Anger is an emotion that can be used for good or evil ends. It can drive us towards the rocks or towards the open seas of accomplishment. It has been defined as 'the instinct of self-protection and the protection of others'. It causes us to stand up and fight against harmful enemies of the personality. When we become angry with evil, we stiffen ourselves against it and oppose it. Otherwise we would allow it to invade us and others. Jesus was an example of anger rightly used. When he was about to heal the man with the withered arm he saw the hardened faces of the religious men who opposed his act of mercy because it was done on the Sabbath. He looked at them 'with anger, grieved at their hardness of heart' (Mark 3:5 rsv). His anger was not personal pique at what was happening to him—a wounded egotism—but grief at the hardness of men's hearts that could block the healing of a man who was crippled and infirm. His anger drove him to oppose these men on behalf of the underprivileged. It was, therefore, a righteous anger.

'Anger is righteous,' says Dr E. Stanley Jones, 'if it has in it grief on account of what is happening to others and not a grudge on account of what is happening to oneself.' If we are angry because something didn't go the way we expected, or because our pride has been wounded, then that anger is unrighteous. If we are angry, however, because of some injustice done to another, or because of some sin that dishonours the name of Christ, then that anger is righteous. But we must be careful when differentiating between righteous and unrighteous anger because the mind plays tricks on itself; it will dress up personal pride in garments of righteous and religious indignation so that it will pass muster before the religious self. Some people fight for 'principle' when really they are fighting because of personal pique or pride.

At the heart of all unrighteous anger is self-centredness. Many blame their anger on their circumstances: a boring job, a small house, difficult children, a poor neighbourhood, insufficient finances or interfering in-laws. The real problem, however, is the human ego which wants unrestrained freedom to do whatever it pleases, expecting at the same time the love and approval of one's partner. The human ego, unless firmly surrendered to Jesus Christ, has within it a strong propensity for wanting its own way. It wants to be the sun around which its partner orbits as a devoted planet. 'If such planets would vie for centrality in the same solar system,' says a scientist, 'the result would be chaos.' That is exactly what happens in many marriages.

'If you are angry, be sure that it is not a sinful anger. Never go to bed angry—don't give the devil that sort of foothold' (Ephesians 4:26–27 PHILLIPS). Unless the will of both husband and wife are totally submitted to Jesus Christ, then unrighteous anger can soon take control. David Augsburger puts his finger on the problem of unrighteous anger being basically due to self-centredness when he says: 'Anger is a demand that you hear *me*, that you stop violating *my* rights…that you stop trying to control *my* life…that you recognize *my* wrath….that you leave *me* alone to do whatever *I* please.' He goes on to say that before unrighteous anger arises in your heart you first feel anxiety—a sign that your self-esteem or self-regard is endangered. 'When your "freedom" to be you is threatened,' he says, 'you become anxious, tense and ready for action. What type of action? Usually a hostile and bitter one.'

Whenever you next feel unrighteous anger arising within your heart, whatever you do, don't repress it and pretend it is not there. Instead accept its presence and say to yourself: 'I'm feeling angry.' Some people think to themselves, 'I shouldn't be angry; it's unspiritual,' so they push the emotion of anger back down inside themselves. But you never bury an emotion dead—you always bury it alive—and then it works in the subconscious in an unhealthy and unproductive way. Admitting you feel angry is not saying you agree with it. By accepting its presence you bring it out into the open where you can deal with it. It's a psychological law that before you can deal with any problem you must first admit it is there.

Next ask yourself: 'Why am I angry? What has happened to cause this anger within me? What part of my ego has been pricked? How has my pride been hurt?' Try to discover the cause of your anger. Then set about controlling it. You can do this best by quietly confessing to the Lord that you are angry, and asking his forgiveness for reacting wrongly to the situation. When you have done this, ask for his help in bringing your anger under control. You'll be surprised how quickly the Holy Spirit comes alongside a Christian who, overwhelmed by feelings of anger, appeals to the Lord for help. You don't have to pray a long prayer to get the Lord's help in controlling your anger. Remember one of the shortest prayers in the Bible was prayed by Simon Peter when he was sinking in the lake of Galilee: 'Lord, save me.' It had Christ at one end, himself at the other and salvation in between. And the Lord who saved Peter from drowning in the depths of Galilee can also save you from being engulfed in the deep, dark waters of unrighteous anger. So control your anger. With a committed will and God's help—it's possible.

Focus on tackling the conflict—not each other

It may be difficult in the heat of emotional upheaval to stop and carefully define what it is that is upsetting you. But then I am assuming you are a Christian committed to taking God's way rather than your own in the matter of resolving conflicts. And God's way lays great stress on personal responsibility. And, remember, God never asks us to do anything that demands personal effort without supplying us with the grace and power to accomplish it.

When a conflict arises within your marriage, write down, if you can, what is troubling you—in one or two sentences if possible—as this will help clarify the heart of the issue. The more narrowly and precisely a problem is defined, the easier will be the solution. In evaluating the core of the conflict you will need to do several things. Consider, for example, your own and your partner's behaviour. How has your behaviour, and that of your partner, contributed to the problem? What behaviour do you think your partner sees as contributing to the problem?

Once you are clear as to what the problem is, then attack the problem—not your partner. It is easy to become over-critical in an argument and make inaccurate character judgements of your partner. We have a tendency to project our own motives onto other people; our angry accusations against our partners often reveal more about our own hearts than about theirs. The apostle Paul made an interesting observation about people who judge others: 'You, therefore, have no excuse, you who pass judgement on someone else...' (Romans 2:1 NIV).

Take, for example, the conflict some wives feel when their husbands leave their personal belongings such as clothes, shaving equipment, etc., strewn all over the house. Many women become angry over this, and say something like, 'For goodness sake—why on earth can't you pick things up after you? I've asked you a thousand times to do this. But it's like water off a duck's back. I'm sick and tired of running around after you, picking up this, that and the other. If you had one ounce of real love for me you wouldn't need to be told more than once. What kind of example are you to the children?'

Now contrast this with a wife who has learned to recognize her anger, control it and deal with the issue in a more biblical way. Approaching her husband at an appropriate time, she says something like this: 'I've got a problem which we must talk about. I feel hurt when you don't pick your things up after you. I'm sorry about these feelings, and I'm working it out with the Lord, but it would help me no end if you could make sure things are picked up when you've finished with them. I could then give more time to the children, to my own devotional reading and times with the Lord...do you think you could help me in this?'

Now this kind of statement does several things:

(a) It demonstrates a Christian commitment to controlling one's anger.

(b) It accepts responsibility for part of the problem: 'I have a problem...'—resentment.

(c) It condenses the conflict into a single sentence: 'I feel resentful at you for not picking your clothes up after you...' (naturally not all conflicts can be narrowed down to a single sentence. But most can.)

(d) It focuses on the problem without projecting blame onto the other person. Doubtless the other person will feel some blame, but this is inherent, not projected.

(e) It asks for a conclusion: 'Do you think you could help me in this way?'

Decide to deal with conflict issues as soon as possible after they occur

Some conflicts which arise in marriage can be dealt with as soon as they arise, but others, because of their nature, may need to be discussed a little later. It's always a good idea to have a cooling-off period for heated emotions to subside, but a matter should never be left long enough for silent resentment to start building up again.

'Let not the sun go down upon your wrath' (Ephesians 4:26). This, in terms of marriage, means being ready and willing to resolve conflicts before one goes to sleep at night. I made that statement recently at a Family Life Seminar in one of Britain's largest cities, and immediately after the session finished, a man came up to me and queried, 'Even if my wife has started the whole problem?' I explained that a man, being the leader of the home and responsible for the climate of love and freedom, must take the initiative in resolving conflicts, even if his wife has started the whole thing. A man's feelings may be so deeply hurt by his wife's attitudes or actions that he may feel disinclined to take any initiative, but at such times he should remind himself of the biblical injunction in Ephesians 5:25, 'Husbands, love your wives, even as Christ also loved the church, and gave himself for it.'

A man should initiate conversation by saying, 'Let's talk.' But be careful not to follow the example of one young husband who, when trying to implement this principle, said to his wife, 'You've been acting like a two-year-old for the past few hours. Come here and let's talk.' He couldn't figure out why this made his wife angrier than she was before!

That husband missed a vital point in attempting to

resolve the conflict—something I touched on earlier—and that is the importance of making 'I' rather than 'you' statements. 'You've been acting like a two-year-old...' is accusatory and puts a person on the defensive. What this husband should have said was something like this: 'I feel there is something wrong between us. If there is anything I have contributed to the problem, then I am prepared to face it. But please, let's talk.' I am pretty sure that although such statements do not always produce the desired result, his wife would have been more receptive to the idea of resolving the issue.

The husband's role of being the leader in a marriage does not, however, absolve a woman from all responsibility in dealing with conflict issues as soon as possible after they occur. If for any reason a man fails to initiate discussion on a serious conflict, the woman must not sit back and excuse herself by saying, 'It's not my function.' While the responsibility for leadership lies with the man, there are many scriptures which show that everyone, irrespective of sex, has a responsibility to clear up conflicts as quickly as possible after they have occurred. Take this one, for example: 'If your brother sins against you, go and show him his fault' (Matthew 18:15 NIV). And, 'If you... remember that your brother has something against you ...go and be reconciled to your brother' (Matthew 5:23–24 NIV). And, 'Settle matters quickly with your adversary who is taking you to court. Do it while you are still with him on the way' (Matthew 5:25 NIV).

In dealing with conflict, pick a time which suits you both, not just before a meal or when someone is going out through the door on the way to work. Naturally the one who feels the need for discussion must be willing to give up a favourite television programme or sacrifice some personal pleasure in the interests of resolving the conflict. A research psychologist, who studied several hundred couples with a view to finding out how they handled their conflicts, found that, for most, attempting to sort out their problems in the bedroom or the kitchen had psychological disadvantages. In most of the couples researched it was discovered that the best atmosphere for resolving disputes was the living room.

Guard against interruption. You may want to take the phone off the hook or not answer the door. If you have children, ask them not to interrupt you because you are having an important discussion and that you will talk to them when it is finished. Keep in mind also that parents can't succeed in hiding their disagreements from the children. Let them know that sometimes you disagree, and that when there are serious disagreements, immediate steps are taken to resolve them. If you can establish a healthy pattern for conflict resolution in your marriage, it will do a lot to help your children learn to disagree in a healthy way—and this can contribute to peace and harmony in the home.

Be prepared to admit when you are wrong

It takes a good deal of humility to say you are wrong. I can't begin to count the number of times people have told me that the hardest words for them to say to their partner are, 'I'm sorry,' or 'I was wrong.' I usually get such people to practise saying the phrase to themselves a few hundred times, and even then some find it almost impossible to say it to their partner. What is it that makes a Christian man or woman resist admitting they are sorry or that they are wrong? Basically it is pride. When we are about to do something that is spiritually beneficial, it's surprising how pride and self-centredness come to our head under the guise of preventing us from 'making fools of ourselves'. This inward pride needs to be seen for what it is, and firmly renounced in the name of Jesus Christ.

Some Christians compromise on this issue and make

such statements as follows:

> 'I was wrong but so were you, too!'
> 'I'm sorry but you must realize it was not all my fault.'
> 'If I'm wrong then I apologize.'
> 'I'm quite willing to say I'm sorry if you want me to.'

These statements, fine though they may sound, all reflect pride. When you honestly own up to the fact that you were wrong and say so simply and without an element of pride, you improve communication a thousandfold and deepen your relationship with your partner.

Listen to the advice given by the writer of the book of Proverbs centuries ago: 'A man who refuses to admit his mistakes can never be successful. But if he confesses and forsakes them, he gets another chance' (Proverbs 28:13 TLB). Ogden Nash, a modern-day writer, put it succinctly when he wrote:

> To keep your marriage brimming
> With love in the loving cup,
> When you're wrong, admit it,
> When you're right, shut up.

Focus on the solutions, not only on the problems

Begin to work as soon as possible on a mutually agreeable solution. Let's face it—if we worked as hard on producing solutions as we do on delineating our problems, our conflicts would be far fewer. Once each partner has given his or her understanding as to the causes of the conflict, work must then begin on producing mutually acceptable solutions. With the conflict carefully defined and pinpointed, then comes the time for what is called 'brainstorming'. Brainstorming is attacking a problem with a view to coming up with a variety of answers or solutions. Each partner should think of as many solutions

to the conflict as possible. The greater the number of
possible solutions, the more likely you are to find one that
pleases you both.

After listing all of the alternative solutions, make a
short list of the ones you feel have some merit. Then
evaluate them one by one and consider the steps necessary
to put them into effect. If one partner likes one of the
alternative solutions but the other finds it unacceptable,
discuss the reasons. Mutual sharing promotes growth,
providing it is done in a spirit of unity and love.

Solutions to conflict almost invariably demand a change
in behaviour on the part of both partners. Concentrate on
your own behaviour changes and allow your partner to
work on his or hers. An outline that has helped many
people resolve conflicts and come up with alternative
solutions is this:

(a) The conflict between us is _____

_____

(b) Its effect on me is _____

_____

(c) My contribution to this conflict is _____

_____

(d) My proposed solutions are 1. _____

    2. _____   3. _____

    4. _____   5. _____

(e) The agreed, mutually acceptable solution is _____

_____

(f) The change(s) I have to make is (are) _____

_____

One couple who were having continual conflicts in their marriage had several of these 'Conflict Resolution' sheets printed by a local printer so that they were always on hand whenever needed. They told me that after the first few 'fights', however, they dropped into the style of sharing together their feelings and ideas about their problems in a non-hostile manner, coming up with mutually acceptable solutions, so that they no longer needed the forms. Resolving conflicts in this manner became for them a way of life. They also told me that the more conflicts they resolved, the more growth and understanding developed between them, which resulted in fewer and fewer conflicts in their marriage.

For some, of course, this procedure for conflict resolution may seem too structured and artificial. I can only say that hundreds of couples have found that it works. Resolving conflict, remember, is not a matter of winning and losing; by using this conflict-solving approach, both husband and wife find a creative solution that brings satisfaction to both.

End all conflicts by an act of forgiveness

Asking your partner's forgiveness for your own involvement in a marital conflict is one of the most humbling but yet one of the most gratifying things you can experience. Dan Benson in his book *The Total Man* (Tyndale House Publishers) tells most movingly of what he calls 'the magic power of forgiveness'.

> In one of our earliest fights Kathy and I were both too indignant to bother asking or granting forgiveness for each other. We both fumed, silently, for several days afterwards. Then I read something I didn't really want to see. To back up my righteous indignation I was reading the Bible and I came across these words: '...bearing with one another, and forgiving each other, whoever has a complaint against anyone; just as the Lord forgave you, so also should you' (Colossians 3:13 NASB). *Gulp*—it came down to the initiative a leader must take. If the Lord took that initiative to forgive me when I didn't deserve it, then he intends me to take the initiative to restore things with my wife, regardless of whose fault it was. I had been blowing it by letting my pride say, 'She's got to come to me first.' I wandered into the kitchen where Kathy was preparing dinner. 'Honey,' I ventured, cautious of becoming vulnerable, 'I've felt convicted about our fight the other day...I don't think we've finished it.' 'What do you mean?' she said. 'Well, I was wrong for the way I shouted at you. I'm sorry—will you forgive me?' Kathy smiled, put down the dishes and melted into my arms. 'I was just getting ready to ask you the same thing,' she said. 'Yes, I forgive you. Will you forgive me?' 'You bet,' I said.

Some might respond to this illustration by saying, 'That's all right if the problem is superficial, but what about when the hurt goes deep and I can't forgive?' Whenever I am counselling anyone who uses the words, 'I can't,' I suggest to them that during the counselling sessions I am going to introduce a rule which goes like this: the word 'can't' is no longer in our vocabulary and we substitute instead 'won't', or 'haven't learned how to yet'. It is positively staggering the effect this has upon some people.

A woman once said to me, 'I can't forgive my husband,' even after I had introduced the rule. So, remembering what I had said, she caught her breath and said, 'Sorry...I mean I won't forgive my husband or I haven't learned how to yet.' I watched her for a few moments as the realization of what she had said dawned upon her. Bursting into tears, she said, 'What a fool I've been. I've been waiting all the time to feel like forgiving, but I realize now that I will never really feel like it... I have to be willing to forgive.'

She was right. Forgiveness is not a feeling; it is an act of will. And there are serious complications set up in the Christian life if we resist God's command to offer forgiveness to those who have hurt us.

Listen to what Christ said in Matthew 6:14–15, 'Your heavenly Father will forgive you if you forgive those who sin against you; but if *you* refuse to forgive *them, he* will not forgive *you*' (TLB). At first glance this seems to be saying that our own forgiveness is based on our forgiveness of others, instead of on God's grace as expressed through Jesus Christ. However, this would contradict Christ's other teachings. I believe that what the Scripture is teaching here is this—if we refuse to forgive the person who has wronged us, we have failed to realize the full effect of God's forgiveness in our own lives. God's forgiveness is ours the moment we repent of our sin and receive Christ, but the full realization of the forgiveness only comes as we decide by an act of will to forgive those who have offended us. Paul, the apostle, put it this way: 'Be gentle and forbearing with one another and, if one has a difference (a grievance or a complaint) against another, readily pardoning each other; even as the Lord has freely forgiven you, so must you also (forgive)' (Colossians 3:13 AMP.).

What is Christian forgiveness? It might be easier to understand if we consider what it is not. Forgiveness is *not* forgetting. Nothing that happens to us is ever really forgotten. It may sink down into our subconscious and be difficult to recall, but it is never really forgotten. When we forgive, all the details of the offence live on in our memory, but the feelings of bitterness and resentment that surround those details are siphoned off in the act of forgiveness. We can still remember it, but emotionally it no longer affects us.

Forgiveness is *not* pretending. Some people attempt to deal with an offence by pretending it never happened, but what has been done is done. Wishing it never happened will never alter the fact. Forgiveness is not a feeling, as we have seen, but an act of the will. It is clear, logical action taken by the will that says to the thoughts and feelings: 'The matter is now over—I forgive in Jesus' name.'

Forgiveness is not bringing up the past. One writer says that many Christians carry in their hearts a trading stamp book with unlimited pages. For each hurt they receive, they lick a stamp and paste it in. When the right time comes, they trade in those stamps and turn them into destructive anger.

Finally, forgiveness is not demanding a person to change before we forgive. To do this reveals our own faithlessness. If you say to a person, 'I will forgive if you change or promise never to do it again,' then you are not really practising forgiveness.

Christian forgiveness is wiping the slate clean. It is self-giving without self-seeking. It is also extremely costly and substitutional. James O. Buswell in his book *A Systematic Theology of Christian Religion* (Zondervan) says, 'All forgiveness, human and divine, is in the very nature of the case vicarious, substitutional, and this is one of the most valuable views my mind has ever entertained. No one ever really forgives another, except he bears the penalty of another's sin against him.'

Remember, time does not heal wounds. Only forgiveness can do that. Conflicts are never fun, but Christian couples must know better than to allow the inevitable conflicts of marriage to push them further and further apart. Decide right now to settle on a set of rules ahead of time (if the ones I have given do not suit you, then build your own), and when conflict arises deal with it as quickly as possible.

Now using what we have said over the past two chapters on communication and conflict resolution in marriage, let's pull many of the things we have looked at into perspective to form what we will call a *peace pact*. If it helps, make it your own manifesto:

When conflicts arise in our marriage, we will:

View it as something that can contribute to the growth and development of our marriage. Instead of saying, 'Oh, not again,' and allowing ourselves to become depressed by it, we will take the setback and turn it into a springboard—and use it to build a better marriage.

Recognize any anger that arises within us and, with God's help, seek to bring it under control. We know that because we are not fully-fledged saints, but saints in the making, anger is going to arise, but when it does we shall admit it, and ask for the Holy Spirit's assistance in bringing it under control.

Deal with conflicts as soon as possible after they occur, allowing a reasonable time to cool down, and before we go to sleep at night. It may not always be convenient and one of us may have to sacrifice some personal interest in resolving the issue, but to the best of our ability, we will make this our goal.

Pinpoint the conflict and reduce it to one or two sentences, so that the issue is clear in both our minds. We will stubbornly refuse to allow irrelevant factors to intrude into the argument, and put up a fence around the conflict issue so that it can be dealt with as quickly and as effectively as possible.

Attack the problem and not the person, We will work on this to the best of our ability, assuring our partner that we love them even though we may be in disagreement over a certain issue.

Avoid projecting blame on to the other person, but accept responsibility for our own contribution to the conflict. This means that we will have to use, 'I feel...' or 'I am...' statements more often. The words, 'You *never...*' are no longer in our vocabulary.

Focus more on creating solutions than on delineating problems. This means brainstorming the issue until we come up with alternative solutions. Then when we have agreed on a mutual solution, we will consider what changes of behaviour each one of us needs to make, then implement them right away. We will concentrate on changing ourselves, rather than on changing our partner.

Listen perceptively and seek to understand not only the thoughts but the feelings of our partner. As feelings are the channel through which everyone best communicates, we will use this channel to both share and understand.

Develop the ability to say 'I was wrong' or 'I am sorry' and use it when appropriate. We recognize that these words are difficult for our carnal nature to accept, but because we are committed to God's way in resolving our conflicts we are determined to crucify the flesh and let God's Spirit have his way in our hearts.

Be sure to seek forgiveness and also give it. This we regard as the most important challenge, as it determines whether we are merely lowering the flame under the cooker or turning the current off completely. Even if I was only one per cent wrong, I still need to ask forgiveness for that percentage.

Follow this Peace Pact when you come up against marital conflict, and, I promise you, it will help turn every problem into a possibility—the possibility of deeper union and more meaningful relationships.

5

PARENTS AND IN-LAWS

'I'm fed up with the way his mother interferes in our marriage,' Betty said angrily. 'She just can't leave us alone.' Before I could say a word, Betty began to list her grievances. 'She criticizes everything I do. If it's not my cooking, it's the way I handle the children. And what irritates me most is not just what she says, but the way she says it. She is pompous, arrogant and talks down to me. How can anyone respect a woman like that?'

Betty, a 28-year-old ex-schoolteacher and housewife, and her husband Tony, had recently joined my church in central London. One day, after reading in the church bulletin that I was available for counselling, they came to see me to discuss the difficulty Betty was having with her mother-in-law.

'How do you feel about the situation?' I asked Tony. 'Well,' he said, 'I'm between the devil and the deep blue sea. I want to take my wife's side, but then doesn't the Bible teach us to honour and obey our parents? I don't know what to do really.'

As I listened to Betty and Tony that day, I remember reflecting on the fact that had someone given them some good pre-marital counselling, the chances are that they would have been able to handle their parent and in-law problems without the necessity of seeing a counsellor.

Good pre-marital counselling would have brought the issue of parent and in-law relationships out into the open, so that any potential problems could be identified and guidelines given for dealing with problem issues in a proper and biblical manner. Whenever I counsel couples prior to their marriage, they usually smile when I bring up the issue of parent and in-law relationships. But more often than not, one year after the wedding, they make it a point to thank me for taking the time to pinpoint the potential problems.

Generally speaking, society is unkind to the members of what is called 'the extended family'—especially mothers-in-law. Jokes about mothers-in-law seem to be one of the most popular forms of entertainment. Gordon and Dorothea Jack, co-authors of the book *I Take Thee,* have this to say concerning mothers-in-law: 'There is perhaps no other cultural stereotype as powerful. The bad press which mothers-in-law receive caricature them as selfish, malicious and interfering. Rarely are they seen as unselfish, thoughtful and considerate persons.' Someone suggested a solution: 'Outlaw the in-laws!' But it is not as simple as that. Not all families have trouble with their in-laws, of course. I know many families who have good and happy relationships with them. A friend of mine, now gone to be with the Lord, used to refer to his mother-in-law as a 'mother-in-love'. His was a happy relationship indeed.

Studies into the subject of in-law relationships have come up with some interesting information. One research psychologist claims (and his findings agree with many other studies) that most in-law problems are predominantly feminine— a wife and her husband's mother in particular. Rarely do the male members of two families find themselves at odds. The reason for in-law problems being mostly between women is attributed to the fact that society is in the main male-dominated, and so the women are forced to compete for the favour and attention of men. If men reinforce this dominance by permitting the women to compete, then this of course greatly complicates the problem. A wife seeks the favour and attention of her husband and so, of course, does his mother.

Another factor appears to be that a wife usually feels insecure as she approaches marriage, and wonders whether she will be adequate in her new role. This sense of inadequacy gives rise to feelings of competition, as she reflects on whether she will be able to do as well for her husband as his mother did. This feeling is seldom discussed, but it is most definitely there. And if a young wife is not aware of what is happening inside her, it can put a pressure on her that can cause an in-law problem. As one writer points out, 'This competition is really unfair, for it's between a novice and a woman who has been meeting the man's needs for more than twenty years.'

Yet another reason for pressure falling upon the ladies is the fact that the marriage of a child is far more threatening to a mother than to the father. The father's life does not revolve so much around the children. Sometimes when a child gets married, a mother experiences great trauma, and reaches out for something that will enable her to maintain meaning. The father has his work which takes up a lot of his time and attention, and because he normally works outside the home, the problem of adjustment for him is less acute. If a man is insensitive to what his wife is going through at this stage, this can complicate the problem even more, causing the mother to vie with her daughter-in-law for her son's attention.

A further factor that might explain the difficulties which arise between female in-law relationships is the way in which women express their feelings and deal with conflicts. Men are inclined to confront each other openly when there are problems, thus bringing them out into the open where they can be discussed and resolved. Women, how-

ever, tend to express themselves in less obvious ways.
Conflicts between women can reverberate beneath the
surface for days, weeks, or even months, until they finally
explode. Then the men react in one of two ways—either
stepping in and trying to resolve the problem, or ignoring
it and hoping it will resolve itself.

It might be helpful if in this chapter I shared with you
some of the guidelines I give to engaged couples on the
subject of parent and in-law relationships. They apply
equally well to those who have been married for some
time.

Leave, cleave and become

First, seek to understand what exactly is involved in God's
command to leave, cleave and become one flesh.

In Genesis 2:24 God describes marriage in this way:
'For this cause a man shall leave his father and his mother,
and shall cleave to his wife; and they shall become one
flesh' (NASB). Notice the three verbs in this statement—
'leave', 'cleave', and 'become'.

Walter Trobisch has written at great length on the
importance of these three verbs. He suggests that *leaving*
is not something merely geographical, moving away from
the parental home, but something that is psychological—
breaking away from the original parental ties. And this,
he points out, is exactly what many married couples fail to
do. Socially, they enter into a wedding ceremony, but
psychologically they are not prepared to move from one
relationship to another. The word 'leave' does not mean,
of course, that a couple now abandon their parents and
show no more concern or interest in them. What it means
is that the couple move out from under the authority of
their parents to establish for themselves a new authority
structure. Marriage is intended to be, in part, a clean
break with the former parental relationship, in which the

couple say, in effect, 'Here at this moment our loyalty and authority change hands. From now on our highest commitment is to each other.'

Only those who work with troubled marriages know how serious can be the repercussions if a couple fail to 'leave' their parents in the true sense of the word. When one member of the marriage looks back at parental ties, and hankers for the comforts or securities of the parental home, then the relationship becomes uneasy. A husband who wants to maintain an emotional authority relationship with his parents will feel inadequate as a leader. The wife who fails to make a psychological break with her parents will feel insecure and unable to trust her husband's leadership.

If the word 'leave' is a negative word, meaning a parting from former obligations, then the word 'cleave' is a positive one, symbolizing the fact of assertively giving oneself to a new relationship. It means a commitment to hold on and advance against every force or threat which would seek to divide the loyalties and fidelities of the marriage union. Some Hebrew scholars say that the word has a progressive thrust, and suggests a continuum along which a couple must move from day to day. I have counselled scores of couples who thought that the love they both shared on their wedding day was a guarantee that they would love each other for the rest of their lives. But it wasn't, as they came to discover after many heartaches and problems. In my view it's tragic that so many ministers fail to impress upon couples about to be married the fact that love is more than just a feeling; it is a commitment that dedicates itself not to just holding on but to moving the relationship to higher and more meaningful levels.

The phrase 'become one flesh' refers, of course, to the sexual relationship. But it must be pointed out that only when the first two steps have been taken—leave and cleave—does the sexual relationship have its fullest meaning. Some people approach marriage simply in order to be 'one flesh' with their partner—they see marriage as predominantly sexual. Others approach marriage in order to 'cleave' to their partner—they see marriage as merely companionship. And some approach marriage as a way of getting out from under the authority of their parents, or to break with unhappy parent-child relationships. They see marriage simply as 'leaving' a past relationship—an escape route from an unhappy past.

No marriage, however, can be properly established unless the stages come in the scriptural order—leaving, cleaving and becoming one flesh. God intends sex to be more than a physical relationship. It is to be a physical expression of mental, emotional and spiritual intimacy. And there can be no true intimacy in marriage until the steps of leaving and cleaving are examined and understood.

Whenever I counsel couples about to be married, after explaining the meaning of these three important verbs—leave, cleave, and become one flesh—I ask them if they clearly understand the importance of pulling away from the parental relationship and seeing marriage as a point in time when loyalties and authorities change hands. Time and again, couples have been so grateful for having this spelt out; they have told me this one insight alone equipped them to establish a marriage in which their in-laws would have access but not direction and control. If you are having in-law trouble, may I suggest, before you read further, that you examine your own personal position and ascertain whether or not you have put the parental relationship well and truly behind you? I stress again, 'leaving' does not mean abandoning your parents, or being unappreciative of all they have done for you. It simply means that a new structure has to be established and a new way of life developed. We are to honour our parents for a lifetime, but at the point of marriage their authority over us ceases.

Resolve parent-child conflicts

Another guiding principle I share with couples about to be married concerning in-law relationships is this: clear up any unresolved conflicts with your parents before you enter into marriage. Experience has shown that unresolved conflicts between parents and children can be carried over into marriage and will work to undermine the new relationship. If there is animosity, bitterness, anger, or hatred on the part of a son or daughter towards a parent, then it is imperative that this is dealt with before the marriage union takes place.

Alex, a friend of mine I knew in my teens, was brought up in a home by a father who was exceedingly belligerent and angry, and who treated both him and his mother with nothing but contempt. Alex vowed he would never treat his wife or children the way his father had treated him, and often said in my presence, 'I will make sure when I am married that I will never become like my father.' But a year or two after Alex was married, I enquired of his wife, Rachel, how their marriage was working out and she said, 'I don't know what's got into him—he seems just like his father.' I was just a young minister at the time and knew very little about counselling, but one night, at Alex's and Rachel's invitation, I sat with them while they discussed their problems. Unfortunately, at that time, I was unable to help them very much, but if I had known then what I know now, I believe I could have helped them solve their problem.

The key to understanding Alex's difficulties was given to me years later when I came across what someone has called 'the law of the focus of concentration'. This is how it works. Whatever we concentrate on in life, we tend to become like. Alex had a focus of hatred towards his father—a focus revealed in the words, 'I will never become like my father.' So great was his focus of hatred that the next thing that happened was that he became much like his father in his root attitudes. No, he didn't shout and rave and get drunk, but he took on the basic attitudes of his father which were disrespect and lack of genuine love. The focus of concentration (which in his case was one of hate) caused him to identify with the root attitudes of his father, so much so that although he didn't manifest quite the same behaviour as his father, yet he possessed the same inner attitudes. He became like him.

If I was counselling Alex today I would encourage him to get rid of his bitterness and hatred towards his father by putting into operation the principle of forgiveness. I would explain to him that the 'law of focus of concentration' was making him into the same image as the person he hated. Remember this law says that 'you become like the thing or person you hate'. You might not have that person's outer characteristics, but you will most certainly identify and copy their root attitudes. Ever since I discovered this law at work in human life, I have encouraged couples about to be married to make sure that they have a clear conscience on all matters affecting their relationship with their parents —before leaving home.

A letter of appreciation

Another suggestion I make in this area of parental and in-law relationships is for the couple to write to their parents, thanking them for the way they were brought up and for the lessons they learned from them. One couple I counselled on this point said they couldn't think of anything to appreciate about their parents, and could they be excused from this aspect of the pre-marital counselling sessions? I took a firm line with them and said that I wouldn't excuse them from the issue, but I would work with them to help them identify issues that were deserving of appreciation. 'What about the times they looked after you when you

were sick?' I said. 'And the meals they made for you....?
There must be at least a dozen things that as you look back
over your life you can say thank you for!'

My prompting succeeded in opening up a flood of
memories for them both. It's amazing how things come to
mind whenever we set about the task of recalling items in
our family history for which we can give honest and sincere
praise. I was present at the wedding reception of this
couple where the fathers of the bride and groom said
publicly that they would treasure all the days of their life
the letters of appreciation they had received from their
children. This suggestion (not originally mine) has brought
more positive results in building good parent and in-law
relationships than any other single idea I have known.

Your marriage is private

Another guiding principle I encourage couples to follow
in relation to their parents and in-laws is this: protect the
privacy of your marriage and gently resist any outside
interference from your parents or parents-in-law.

Living with in-laws or having them live with you can put
undue strain on any family. I realize, of course, that there
are times when this is unavoidable, but it is best, whenever
possible, for a couple to set up home independently of
their parents. On several occasions I have encouraged
couples to postpone their wedding plans for a while so
that they could work towards setting up an independent
unit in their own flat or rented rooms.

Bill and Hilda, a young couple I once took through a
pre-marital counselling course, told me that because of
their circumstances they would have to spend the first
year of their married life with Bill's parents. I suggested a
postponement and although they said they saw the wisdom
of that advice, they still felt they ought to go ahead with
their marriage plans. They asked me, however, to help

them work out some guidelines for handling their relationship with Bill's parents, and the following is what resulted from our discussions together. Bill and Hilda sat down with his parents and went over these points one by one, and lovingly asked for their agreement and understanding. I realize these guidelines might not work for everybody, but as they worked in this case it may be helpful to reproduce them here.

1. While appreciative of the offer to set up our own family unit in your home, we are deeply aware of the need for privacy so that we can experience the 'cleaving' of which the Scripture speaks. Your co-operation in giving us the privacy we need to grow and develop in our marriage relationship will be deeply appreciated.

2. We will be grateful for any advice you feel you want to give us, but we must be free to accept or reject advice as we think best. If we reject your advice it does not mean we reject you. In order to keep our relationship happy this must be clearly understood.

3. Doubtless there will be times when we, as a new husband and wife, will disagree and perhaps even quarrel. At such times we would appreciate it if you would recognize our need to resolve our own relationship problems in the way and at the time we think best.

4. If you feel there are times when criticism is needed, then we would be grateful if you will address the criticism to the one concerned and not to the other partner. If criticism is to be directed to us both, then we would appreciate it if it was done when we are together.

5. In seeking to develop our independence, there may be occasions when we might not appear to appreciate your love and concern for us. We would now, therefore, like to place on record our deep appreciation of your love, and would ask for your understanding and patience as, in seeking to establish our independence, we might make mistakes.

Those who have already set up home and find that, through an emergency or a sickness, they are obliged to have their parents or parents-in-law live with them, would do well to establish a time limit, so that the situation does not get out of hand. I know many couples who have taken in their parents to live with them, only to find that their own relationship has suffered as a result. I do not think it is possible to lay down a hard and fast rule and say, 'Never live with your parents or in-laws, and never permit them to live with you.' It works for some but not for others. Whenever I have to counsel a couple who are having problems because of living with their parents or in-laws, or because their parents or in-laws are living with them, I study the situation as it is. If I feel that the couple's marriage is imperilled, then I usually advise that they must take the steps necessary to reinforce their marriage, even if it means a parent or in-law being cared for in a nursing home or hospital. Although it is hard to make rules, there is one rule that ought to be made and kept: a marriage must be protected. Creation orders it.

The husband-wife relationship

Another guiding principle for pursuing good parent and in-law relationships is to develop good relationships between yourselves.

Although potential problems exist in any in-law relationship, far too many couples blame their in-laws for their difficulties when in reality the blame may be largely theirs. 'Usually the same personality traits that create or contribute to in-law problems,' says Paul Fugelberg, 'also cause other kinds of problems within a marriage.'

A married couple who do not have a good relationship with one another will often have a bad relationship with their in-laws, regardless of how their in-laws behave. So run down this checklist and put a *yes* or a *no* against each one as appropriate. Then take the *no* statements and spend time discussing with your partner what you can do to improve.

Can I communicate effectively?   _____

Do I deal with conflicts as they arise, being
   careful not to 'simmer' for days?   _____

Have I a positive self-image?   _____

Can I be assertive: i.e. stand up for what
   I believe to be right, and yet do it in
   a loving manner?   _____

Am I able to take criticism without
   allowing it to devastate me?   _____

Am I a suspicious person?   _____

Protect your marriage against outside interference

Yet another guiding principle to help maintain good relationships between parents and in-laws is this: present a united front to any attempts by parents or in-laws to interfere in your marriage.

Dr David Mace in his book *Getting Ready for Marriage* says, 'When a husband and wife have an agreed policy and stand firmly together putting it into effect, attempts at exploitation and manipulation invariably fail. But any weakness, any crack in the unity of husband and wife, enables the in-laws to drive a wedge in between.' The attitude couples should adopt is one of friendliness but firmness. Make it clear to all concerned that while you want to work for harmony between the generations, you will simply not tolerate unwarranted interference in your marriage. This must be made unmistakably clear and no compromise tolerated.

A couple I once knew, Dennis and Margaret, who were having a good deal of parent and in-law interference, decided to take my advice and confront their parents and

their eyes. This will help you to see things in a different perspective.

6. A woman criticized by her in-laws when her husband is not present should say, 'I think you had better talk to — (naming her husband) about that.' If they persist, she should say, 'I'm sorry you feel that way, but let's leave it there for the moment. You can talk to — about it when you next see him.'

7. It is the husband's responsibility to approach his parents or in-laws in order to bring about the resolution of a conflict. As the leader in the home, the man is given special grace by God to handle difficulties. But remember, grace comes only when you need it. You might feel weak and inadequate to deal with issues, but as you fulfil your role, the strength and firmness you need to handle the issue will flow from God to you—providing, of course, that you approach the issue in a spirit of love, not hostility.

8. Look upon all parent or in-law conflicts not as a groaning point but as a growing point. As we saw earlier in the chapter on communication and conflict resolution, problems, if handled correctly, serve to deepen not destroy relationships.

9. Rehearse and plan what you are going to say to your parents or in-laws about the problem. Reduce it to a minimum number of words. Remember the story of the prodigal son. He rehearsed what he was going to say until he was clear as to his approach. So must you.

10. Deal with the issue as soon as possible after it has arisen. The longer you allow the problem to fester, the greater the possibility of bitterness and resentment eroding your relationship.

11. Let your parents or in-laws know the aspects of the relationship you are pleased about before sharing the problem that concerns you. It is always better to say, 'I am happy about this,' before saying, 'I am not happy about that.'

12. Select an appropriate time to deal with conflict issues. See Proverbs 15:23. Don't telephone your parents or in-laws when they are in bed or might possibly be in the middle of a meal. In any case, a face-to-face approach is best.

The rewards for making the effort to establish harmonious relationships with parents and in-laws are immeasurable. Parents have a wisdom and maturity from which younger couples especially can profit. (Remember, they had in-laws too!) Usually it's worth all the trouble one has to take to build good relationships. They will then be truly *in* and not out of our lives.

6

THE
BIGGEST SINGLE OBSTACLE

Whenever I speak in churches or seminars on the subject of the Christian family and have some time at the end of my talk to deal with questions, the one question which comes up time after time is this: what in your opinion is the biggest single obstacle to a happy and successful Christian marriage? My reply usually takes this form: *attempting to meet your basic personal needs in and through your marriage partner*. This normally brings a spate of further questions such as: 'But isn't it legitimate to have one's needs met in marriage?' 'Isn't that what marriage is for?' 'Doesn't mutual dependency—both partners being obliged to meet each other's needs—create the right atmosphere for marriage?'

At this point I have to explain what I mean by the term 'basic personal needs', and when this is understood, I usually find that the point I am making is accepted and understood. Let me try in this chapter to put my thinking on this subject into some kind of perspective. I'm going to have to integrate some psychological principles with spiritual truth in order to make my meaning clear, but I'll do my best to simplify things and avoid jargon. This chapter may be difficult to absorb but, take my word for it, the truths I am dealing with here can—if acted upon— make a world of difference to your marital relationship.

Let's begin by taking an overall view of the subject of human needs. This is best understood, I believe, by looking at the simple structure developed by Abraham Maslow. He suggested that every human being has five levels of need, and that the lowest one on the hierarchy has to be met before a person is motivated to reach for the one above it.

1. *Physical:* every human being needs air, water, food, warmth, etc., to stay alive, and unless these needs are met then a person cannot continue to live out a physical existence on earth.

2. *Safety:* 'Every person,' says Maslow, 'needs to feel that he will be able to get his physical needs met with the minimum of trouble. If in attempting to get his physical needs met, he encounters danger, he will become anxious and deeply insecure. Security-needs have to do with freedom from danger; some reasonable confidence that physical needs will be met tomorrow.'

3. *Love:* this is the need every human being has to be wanted, cared for, listened to, accepted and understood.

4. *Purpose:* the need to make a significant impact upon one's environment by contributing to society in a meaningful way.

5. *Self-actualization:* the expression of one's highest qualities—giving oneself to others to the fullest extent of one's being.

The principle underlying Maslow's theory is that people are not motivated to meet the 'higher' needs until the 'lower' ones have been met. Thus the higher needs rest on the lower ones, as shown in the diagram below/opposite/overleaf.

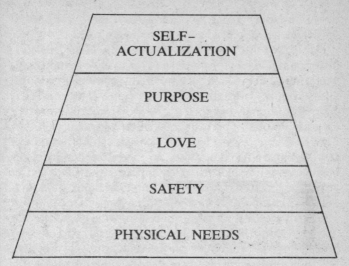

If you have no food in the house, you will be more concerned about getting something to eat today than thinking about what you are going to eat tomorrow. And if you had no idea of where you are going to get food tomorrow, you would hardly be excited at the arrival of a letter from an old friend who said that he thought about you and cared for you a great deal (level 3). Or, to climb to a higher level on Maslow's hierarchy (level 4), you wouldn't be interested, I imagine, in attending a meeting at a local church to hear a famous Bible teacher expound on the subject of 'how to discover your basic spiritual gift'.

Maslow, in introducing this theory, sought to show that we are unable to function effectively at one level until our needs have been met on a lower level. Before we can be fully actualized beings (i.e. beings who are well-adjusted to live out life to its fullest potential), we must pass through the first four stages of need. Maslow's list of needs suggests that safety is a more basic need than love or purpose, because if I am uncertain about where and how I am going to get food tomorrow then I will not be motivated to attempt to meet these higher needs.

I disagree with Maslow on two aspects. First, I do not believe it is possible for a human being to have his personal needs fully met through a mere human relationship alone; and secondly, I do not believe a person can be a fully actualized human being, free from egocentric interests, unless he has had a personal encounter with Jesus Christ. Lawrence Crabb says, 'Maslow's concept of a fully actual-ized human being comes close to the biblical concept of becoming mature in Christ, developing in ourselves those attributes which characterize the Lord and then expressing our God-given worth in freely worshipping God and in serving others by the exercise of our spiritual gifts.' But no one, no matter how good his emotional adjustment, or how happy his childhood, can become a fully expressive and fully functioning person outside of a relationship with God and his Son Jesus Christ.

Having said that, the theory that a human being has certain basic needs which cry out to be met, and that a person is inwardly motivated to meet those needs is, in my view, true to life and in harmony with Scripture. Adam and Eve, prior to the Fall, lived in such a relationship with God that they had need for nothing. In touch with the Almighty and linked to him in a sinless relationship, they were secure and significant individuals with a strong sense of self-worth. When they sinned, however, and were separated from God, the attributes of security, significance and self-worth turned into needs. Security became inse-curity, significance became insignificance, and self-worth became inferiority. The position is that, ever since Adam and Eve's transgression, instead of human beings arriving in the world as God intended—secure, significant and with a solid sense of self-worth—they begin their journey through life with a high deficit. And because God has made every human being with the capacity and potential to be secure, significant and with a sense of self-worth, there is in every human heart a strong desire to regain what has been lost and to become what the inner design of their being beckons them to become.

Let me now bring each of these basic needs into closer focus. The need for security is the need to be loved. There is nothing that meets the need for security more than knowing that someone loves you and takes an active interest in your welfare. The need for significance is the need we have to make an impact on our world by contributing to it through our own uniqueness and individual gifts. The need for self-worth is the need to see ourselves in the eyes of someone else as a person of value. John Powell says of this need,

> It is so essential and so fundamental that if it is met everything else will almost certainly harmonize in a general sense of well-being. When this need is properly nourished, the whole human organism will be healthy and the person will be happy. This need is a true and deep appreciation of oneself, a genuine and joyful self-acceptance, an authentic self-esteem, which results in an interior sense of celebration. It is good to be *me*.

I believe that these three basic personal needs are embedded deep in man's spirit and require a relationship with God before they can be fully met. Of course, a loving relationship with one's parents during the developmental years can go a long way to meeting them. If, for example, parents love their children deeply and make them feel they really 'belong', then they grow up feeling, to some degree at least, a sense of security. If, again, parents train their children to make an impact upon their world by directing them towards the expression of their own uniqueness and the development of their innate abilities, then they enjoy deep feelings of significance. And if they see in the eyes of their parents, admiration and esteem for them as people, not for what they can achieve, but for what they are in themselves, they develop a healthy sense of self-worth.

The problem, of course, is that neither our parents nor we ourselves can adequately meet those basic personal needs, and unless we know how to let God meet them through an ongoing relationship with his Son Jesus Christ, then we go through life trying to meet them ourselves or get others to meet them. For—and this is an important point—if those needs are not met by Christ, then you will unconsciously attempt to get others to meet them. Some people are drawn towards marriage because they unconsciously feel that a partner has the potential of meeting one of their basic needs which hitherto has not been met. If a man's need for security, for example, has not been met in Christ, then, in seeking a marital partner, he may look for someone on whom he can depend. This dependency may appear to be satisfactory for a time, but what happens when, shortly after marriage, he discovers that his partner is just like himself—insecure?

Norman H. Wright says,

> Some of us enter adulthood with needs that were not adequately met in childhood, such as love, security and belonging. Often these early unmet needs freeze into rigid behaviour patterns and enter our marriage with us. Our adult behaviour is then based upon those unmet needs from our childhood. These are called *frozen* needs. They are like recordings that play over and over. And frozen needs cannot be met in the present.

Someone has said: 'Unless a person experiences complete personal fulfilment in Jesus Christ, then he is not free to live for something or someone else.' Can you see what this writer is saying? A person who does not know how to let Christ meet his basic needs for security, significance and self-worth, will be inwardly motivated to meet them on his own, through other people, or in a certain type of behaviour.

Hugh Missildine, in his book *Your Inner Child of the Past,* points out that when a child's sense of self-worth is not properly met in a loving relationship with his parents, then sometimes the child can develop a pattern of behaviour known as 'perfectionism'. He describes such behaviour in this way:

> The perfectionist has real trouble in finding an acceptable marriage partner for he wants a 'perfect' mate not a human one. Thus he tends to reject potential mates, often until he has delayed marriage for years. He has difficulty in forming a relationship that would be close enough to lead to marriage. Some such persons give up the attempt to form close human ties and devote themselves to work, not realizing it lies within their power to alter their attitude toward themselves. The perfectionist looks upon marriage as another achievement. Once married he does not know how to enjoy it. He becomes anxious if the house is not in order at all times, with eggs done to a split-second three minutes, toast to a certain shade of tan, and perfect children from his perfect wife. His anxiety leads him to demand these things because anything less than what he considers 'perfect' arouses his childhood patterns of self-bewilderment.

Theoretically, every Christian is in a position to be free from an inner motivation to meet his basic personal needs by himself, by relating to Christ in such a way that *he* meets them—fully and eternally. It is a sad reflection, but one that can be shown to be true, that many Christians live out their lives no differently from non-Christians, whose main preoccupation in life is getting their needs met in self-centred ways. We sing such songs as: 'Complete, complete, complete in Him; we are complete in him,' and while the words buzz around in our heads, they never really reach our hearts. We give mental credence in church to the belief that Christ is able to meet all our needs, but the moment we get outside, we live no differently from the self-seeking worldling.

What we must do is to focus on the truth of Scripture until the truth grips us not merely in our heads but in our hearts. Lawrence Crabb when writing about Maslow's hierarchy of needs says, 'The Christian is to travel through levels 1–4 on the wheels of faith. God has promised to meet all of the needs indicated on Maslow's list.' He then lists the biblical promises for each of Maslow's levels of need:

1. *Physical needs:* 'Seek first his kingdom and his righteousness, and all these things [referring to food, clothing and shelter] will be given to you as well' (Matthew 6:33 NIV).

2. *Safety needs:* 'Therefore do not worry about tomorrow' (Matthew 6:34 NIV).

3. *Love needs:* 'Who shall separate us from the love of Christ? . . . I am convinced that [nothing] will be able to separate us from the love of God that is in Christ Jesus our Lord' (Romans 8:35, 38–39 NIV).

4. *Purpose needs:* 'For we are God's workmanship, created in Christ Jesus to do good works, which God prepared in advance for us to do' (Ephesians 2:10 NIV).

If a Christian allows these verses to enter his personality, by meditating upon them until they are spiritually digested and become part of his inner being, he will be freed from a life of self-concern and will, in Maslow's terms, become a self-actualized person.

I will now use the same principle as Crabb used to relate appropriate scriptures to the three basic personal needs as I have described them—security, significance, and self-worth.

1. *Security:* 'God commendeth his love towards us, in that, while we were yet sinners, Christ died for us'

(Romans 5:8).

2. *Significance:* 'For to me to live is Christ, and to die is gain' (Philippians 1:21).

3. *Self-worth:* 'How precious it is, Lord, to realize that you are thinking about me constantly! I can't even count how many times a day your thoughts turn towards me' (Psalm 139:17–18 TLB).

Sit down with your Bible and search out other scriptures which claim that God has promised to meet your every need. Then turn them into spiritual blood and muscle by meditating on them. Remember, you can only appropriate biblical truth by meditating on it. It is not enough to glance at a spiritual truth from the word of God and say, 'Isn't that exciting?' You must focus on it, assimilate it and absorb it into your spiritual bloodstream, so that the truth is carried to all parts of your personality.

The whole point of my argument is that Christians should never operate from the deficit side of life's ledger but from its credit side. Those who do not know how to let Christ meet their basic personal needs feel and act in ways designed to satiate their unmet desires. And as far as marriage is concerned, such people will tend unconsciously to manipulate their partners by words and behaviour to meet their unmet needs.

Let me highlight this point by an illustration taken from a marital counselling session which took place several years ago. Elaine, a middle-aged woman, came to see me because her doctor had said she was suffering from a psychosomatic illness and needed to talk over her problems with a sympathetic and understanding person. 'What's the biggest area of difficulty in your life?' I asked her. After thinking for several minutes she said, 'It's my husband. He doesn't seem to be interested in what I do or how I look. For example, I cleaned the house from top to bottom the other day, and when he came home he didn't even notice it. Gradually over the months and years, this has got to me and now I'm just not able to cope with it any more.'

After listening to Elaine's problem, when she gave me several other instances of her husband's lack of interest and unconcern, I tentatively made the point that although she would find a good deal of pleasure and happiness in her husband's concern for her, God had arranged a way in which she could live a secure life, even though she did not yet have it. Elaine seemed interested in knowing more, so I shared with her the concept I have shared with you in the pages of this chapter.

'God,' I went on, 'has designed us with three basic needs: the needs for security, significance, and self-worth. It seems to me you are really saying, "I feel insecure when my husband doesn't show interest in me. I need to be loved and feel wanted, and when my husband doesn't give me his approval and show some concern and interest in what I do, it leaves me feeling deeply deprived." Well, actually God can so fill your need for security with himself that although you will still feel concerned about your husband's lack of interest, you will certainly not be shattered by it—as you are now.'

By this time, Elaine was sitting on the edge of her seat. 'Do you mean to tell me that I can live a happy and fairly carefree life even though my husband doesn't change?'

'Yes, that's exactly what I am saying,' I replied.

'Show me how,' was her polite challenge.

I said, 'Let's start by recognizing that God has first claim upon your life. He is your God and Saviour, and although your husband is an important part of your life, God is your first love. Is that correct?'

'Yes,' said Elaine, 'that is true in my experience.'

'Now,' I went on, 'I want you to go home, and the next time you clean the house, or do something that you would expect to be noticed by your husband, do it first for the Lord, and then for your husband. After you have finished whatever it is you will be doing, get down on your knees and tell the Lord you have done it for him first and for your husband next.'

Elaine left the counselling room looking slightly nonplussed, but I sensed that in the near future she was about to make a great discovery. And she did. A week or so later she came back to see me, and as soon as we sat down together in the counselling room, she said, 'The most marvellous thing happened. I can hardly wait to tell you. I did as you said. I got down on my knees after I had cleaned the house and said, "Lord, I have done this for you and my husband, please accept it as my humble effort—in Jesus' name."'

Elaine waited a moment, took a deep breath and went on. 'And then it happened. You know, whenever I heard my minister say in a sermon that God had spoken to him, I used to say to myself, "He imagines it," or, "It's his own thoughts which he mistakes for the voice of God." But as I waited before the Lord in prayer, not knowing what more to say, I suddenly heard the voice of God in my heart as clear as a bell.'

It was my turn now to be on the edge of my seat. 'And what did he say?' I asked.

'He said, "Well done." That was all, but his voice was so unmistakable that it left me trembling.'

'And what was the final result of this?' I enquired.

'Well,' she said, 'that night when my husband came home, I wondered, as I usually do, if he would notice that the house had been cleaned and polished, but once again he showed no signs of noticing. But the amazing thing was this—for the first time *I felt no bitterness or resentment towards him for that*. I had already had God's approval, and although it would have been nice to have heard my husband say he appreciated what I had done, or even that he had noticed it, the situation did not upset me as it once did. How do you explain this?'

'Well, Elaine,' I remarked, 'remember me telling you that God has designed you with three basic needs and that he has also made provision through his Son for those needs to be fully met?'

'Yes,' Elaine interrupted, 'and the three basic needs were security, significance, and self-worth.'

I smiled and went on, 'Well, here is an example of you discovering that when you look to Christ to meet your need for security, you are not then as dependent on your husband as you were before. In fact, this releases your personality from some of the unconscious mechanisms by which you strive to get your husband's approval. I wouldn't be at all surprised if, now the pressure is off, you will find that he will begin to respond differently.'

'Well, at the moment,' said Elaine, 'because I have not been nagging him and trying to get him to say the house looks nice and that I have done a good job, he seems to be somewhat confused.'

'That's because the less pressure you put on him,' I said, 'the more freedom he has to really be the man he ought to be, and for a while he won't know how to cope with the change in you... but pray for him and ask God to use this situation to bring him to the place of personal commitment.'

Elaine had already told me her husband was not a Christian and, as I talked, I sensed again that this might well be a situation through which God could work to bring him to the cross. Elaine left that afternoon to work on some principles in relation to her other basic needs, promising me that she would continue to meditate on the texts I had given her until the truth that she was 'complete in him' moved from her head right into her heart.

A few weeks later, one Monday morning, Elaine telephoned me to say that the previous day her husband had attended church with her and had surrendered his life to Jesus Christ.

'That's wonderful news,' I said. 'How did it happen?'

'Can we come and see you,' said Elaine, 'and then we can share with you what God has been doing in our lives?'

I set up an appointment for a couple of weeks later, and on the day and time arranged, Elaine and her husband Tony walked into my office looking the very picture of happiness. I sat back and listened to their story.

Tony told me that when his wife changed, and no longer nagged or reprimanded him for his lack of interest in her and her activities, he found it extremely difficult to cope with the situation. 'You see,' he said, 'I had built up so many defences against my wife's behaviour—tuning her out, changing the subject and so on—that when these were no longer needed I became disoriented. For a few weeks I just didn't know what to do about it, and then one Sunday morning I said to myself, "I'm sick and tired of the way I have been living. Perhaps this is the day I will find God." I asked Elaine if I could go to church with her, and that morning I walked forward after the sermon and asked the pastor to help me to find God. And I'm happy to say I found him, or rather he found me!'

Elaine broke in at this point and said, 'I can see now how my nagging and attempts to get Tony to love me were draining him dry, and he wasn't free to really give himself to me in the way that deep down he wanted to. When I found my need for security could be met by Christ and that I didn't *need* my husband to make me secure, because in Christ I am *already* secure, this took the pressure off both me and him. I became more interested in giving to him rather than taking from him—and the result was that he came to know the Lord.'

This is not the only occasion I know when a Christian wife has, under God, been influential in bringing her non-Christian husband to Christ by changing her attitudes and behaviour. Time and time again Christian wives have told me that their non-Christian husbands have shown interest in spiritual things when they have taken steps to have their basic personal needs met in Christ and not in and through their marriage relationship. Sometimes a Christian wife will pressurize her non-Christian husband to become a Christian to make her feel more secure. This pressure often amounts to manipulation, and when a person is being manipulated he deeply resents it, for it is an offence to his personality. When a wife knows how to let the Lord meet her needs, then she operates from the credit and not the debit side of life's ledger. She is out to give rather than get. Instead of being at the centre of her world, trying to fill her emptiness, she discovers that Christ fills the entirety of her being, and she no longer strives to get, but delights to give.

An ideal marriage is one in which both partners allow the Lord to meet their basic personal needs. When this is so, then both operate from the motivation to give to each other in ways that will contribute to each other's happiness and help each other draw closer to Christ. Both, having their needs for security, significance and self-worth fully met by the Lord, are free to live not for themselves but for the Lord and for each other. Until that goal is reached, marriage problems can never be fully and finally resolved.

7

WANDERING AFFECTIONS

Several years ago, when being interviewed on a Christian radio programme in the United States on the subject of family problems, I was asked this pointed question: 'Here in the United States statistics show that 30% of women and 50% of men have had an extra-marital sexual relationship since they have been married. We don't know the percentage for the Christian community, but we know it is far higher than it ought to be. What principles do you use in counselling people when they have become involved in an extra-marital affair?'

I don't mind admitting that I had a hard time answering that question. I stumbled through a list of things that sprang immediately to mind, but I felt, as I was speaking, that I was far from coming to grips with the issue. The truth was that my thinking on the subject of extra-marital affairs had not been as deep as on other issues, and my interviewer's question revealed the paucity of my ideas on the subject.

When I returned to the United Kingdom I sat down one day to think through the whole issue of unfaithfulness in marriage. I asked myself such questions as these: what causes people to want to have an affair? How does it usually begin? What steps should a person take when they start to become involved with another person other than their own marriage partner? How should an affair be ended? As things began to crystallize in my mind, I made some notes, and these notes are now the basis for this chapter. I hope they will be as much help to you as they have been to the many people with whom I have shared them in a number of counselling sessions.

The circumstances in which we live today tend to make marital unfaithfulness easier than it was in the past. There is more opportunity for it and less censure when it happens. Take the case of Diana, who told me in a recent counselling session, 'It was a terrible shock to me when I found out about my husband and my best friend. For months now he has been taking her home from the mid-week services in his car, unknown to me, and he has just admitted that they have slept together. The bottom seems to have dropped out of my world. I just don't know what to do.'

Diana was full of mixed emotions—anger, disillusionment, fear, self-pity and despair. She went on to say, 'I never dreamed that this could happen to me.' Words, incidentally, that marriage guidance counsellors hear all too often these days.

Then there was Bob, another counsellee I saw recently, who told me that although he loved his wife deeply, he had become involved in an extra-marital affair. Trouble came to Bob in the form of a shapely secretary who had just been divorced and needed a shoulder to cry on. Listening to his secretary's tale of woe made Bob feel needed. The little talks over coffee, however, led to lunch time and dinner meetings. Then one night, when they both had to work late and were alone in the office, it happened. Bob touched her hand and suddenly she was in his arms. They slept together several times until Bob's conscience could take it no longer, and he came to me asking for my help in breaking the relationship with his secretary. 'I love my wife deeply,' he said. 'How could I allow myself to get involved like this?'

Involvement in an extra-marital affair usually begins with what some counsellors call 'wandering affections'. Unless we know how to cope with this problem, we can soon find ourselves pushed over the edge of propriety into sin. But let's face it: sometime, somewhere most of us meet someone, other than our marriage partner, who causes our heart to miss a beat. A noted psychologist said that married people who do not feel an attraction to someone of the opposite sex (other than their partner) at some time or other, are either less than human or are not telling the truth. This may be an overstatement, but certainly the chemistry that goes on between human beings of the opposite sex is a very real thing and doesn't restrict itself to people who are married to each other.

Feeling one's heart flutter when meeting a person for the first time, and whom one might never meet again, is a problem most of us can cope with, but what happens when one feels a growing and developing attraction towards a member of the opposite sex whom one sees every day or fairly regularly? Let's consider some of the background factors which cause this problem. Most of us spend the years of our youth falling ecstatically in and out of love, experiencing both the rapture and agony involved in finding a life partner. Then one day we make a choice and decide to marry. If we have chosen wisely, then the joys and satisfaction that follow leave us happy and well content. Although there are some who in their youth fall in love with just one person and marry that person, generally people go out with a number of different 'dates'. André Maurois says, 'It is a formidable decision to make when one says, "I bind myself for life: I have chosen; from now on my aim will be, not to search for someone who will please me, but to please the one I have chosen."' Marriage is a deliberate act of will, a commitment, a dedication to a great purpose—the founding of a new unit of society.

Marriage does not mean that we cease to have affection for anyone else. The power to develop a new affection for another person is still there, but somewhat tempered by the marriage commitment. If this were not true, individuals wouldn't be so quick to find another partner when their marriage partner dies. The logical implication of all this is that an affection for another person can arise in one's heart while one is married. How do we guard against such an affection getting the better of us?

Most of my married life I have followed three simple guidelines which have helped me cope with this problem of wandering affections. They have worked for me and I believe, if properly applied, they will work for you too.

How to cope with extra-marital attraction

The first guideline is this: *admit it to yourself whenever you feel a strong attraction to another person.* When we repress an emotion that rises within us without first acknowledging it is there, we allow it to fall back into the subconscious as a powerful force. Admitting its presence robs it of much of its power. This does not mean that you are going to agree with the emotion that is there or go along with it, but as I have said several times in this book—and it bears repeating—you can never begin to deal with any problem emotion until you first admit its existence. And don't think that by admitting the emotion is there, you are going to reinforce it and make it more difficult to handle. It *can* become a bigger problem, of course, if you *continue* to focus on it, and that is why we must come right away to the second step: *turn on the tape recorder of your conscience and play back to the problem emotion the moral imperatives that are recorded there.*

The conscience is like a tape recorder in the sense that it contains the voices of the authority figures who have had some control and influence on your life. It carries the voice of your parents, your schoolteachers and other authority figures, but, in addition, it carries the voice of God. The Almighty has built into your conscience the ability to know right from wrong, and although conscience by itself is not an infallible guide, it has an amazing ability to be able to differentiate between what is right and what is wrong. If you are a Bible-reading Christian, then your conscience will be reinforced by the principles contained in the Bible, making it stronger and even more sensitive to right and wrong.

Whenever you are troubled by wandering affections, bring the emotion to the judgement bar of your conscience and switch on the tape recorder, so to speak. Let it play back to you the voices that spoke to you in the past: of truthfulness, righteousness and morality. Remind yourself also of the moral imperatives which God has directly inscribed upon your conscience as a result of reading his word, the Bible. What about this one, taken from the Ten Commandments: 'Thou shalt not covet thy neighbour's wife' (Exodus 20:17). Or this: 'Abstain from all appearance of evil' (1 Thessalonians 5:22). Some men have told me that, when afflicted with wandering affections they have found great strength in reminding themselves of the words of their marriage vows to 'love her, comfort her, honour, and keep her in sickness and in health; and, *forsaking all other,* keep thee only unto her, so long as ye both shall live'.

I realize that this advice might sound naïve and simplistic to someone caught up in the throes of a strong affection for someone other than their marriage partner, and they might say: 'How can I deal with such a turbulent emotion in such a calm and dispassionate way?' Let's be quite clear about this. There are many who think that a strong affection for someone else other than their marriage partner is something they cannot control. This is a false idea and has been made a convenient excuse far too often for the breaking up of a family and a home. 'What could I do?' said a lady to me once. 'I had fallen so head-over-heels in love with Robert, there was nothing I could do about it.' She was quite wrong, for I believe there was a lot she could do about it *if she really wanted to*.

There is little we can do to change our *feelings*, but there is a lot we can do with the *will*. Marriage, as Maurois reminds us, involves a choice, and the choice we make involves a commitment. As we move on through life, other possibilities occur to us—an attraction for someone else might stir in our heart. We are human and it must be so. But, being human also involves us in responsibilities, in loyalties and consideration for others. Emil Brunner says that marriage is based not so much on love as on fidelity. In a sense he is right, for true love has fidelity at its heart.

No matter how strong the feelings, the will has the power, acting in conjunction with the conscience, to choose between what is right and what is wrong. The will has no power over the emotions. It can't say, for example, 'Now you will feel differently.' What the will can do, however, is to bring the troublesome feeling to the judgement bar of conscience and say, 'Now, listen to this...' then play back to it the moral imperatives which are inscribed upon it.

The third principle is this: *if the problem continues, and you find great difficulty in handling your feelings, then take any steps that are necessary to break off a close association*. This is not always as easy as it sounds, especially if your work or ministry is involved. In my experience, however, it is amazing the insight God gives a person who is totally committed to obeying his word and doing his will. If a person feels they cannot avoid being drawn into the whirlpool of emotional involvement, then the best policy is to get right out of danger. Sometimes (not always) this calls for drastic action, as in the case of Betty, a lady I counselled some years ago. Betty found herself greatly attracted to the minister who came to take over the church where she and her husband worshipped. The minister was a widower in his early forties, and a strong and delightful personality. Betty put into operation all the advice I gave her in trying to cope with her feelings for the minister, but, after a year of hard struggle, she confessed that she was unable to conquer it. After a frank discussion with her husband, who was greatly sympathetic to her problem, they decided to move out of the area and find fellowship in another church. Drastic? Well, maybe. But Betty and her husband were able to rebuild their relationship free from the problem she had faced; and after about a year she completely overcame her difficulty. Sometimes, and *always as a last resort,* severe steps may have to be taken to conquer an illicit affection.

What happens, however, when an attraction for a person passes from being one-sided: the two people concerned acknowledge the mutual feelings they have for one another? Well, it is highly unlikely that they can revert to the type of relationship they had before their feelings were made known, and the only sensible course is to make a clean break. This action is always painful, and the deeper the relationship has been allowed to go, the sharper will be the pain. The break is usually followed by a period of great heartache and misery, but when the resolution has been wholehearted and sincere, the Lord begins at once the process of healing.

As a pastor for many years, I have nursed a number of people through the various stages of heartache that follow the break-up of an association such as I have been describing. However, I have *always* found that the commitment to do what is right, even though one's feelings scream out against it, brings an inner fortitude and a sense of God's presence that carries a person through to final victory.

Dealing with the sin of adultery

So far, I have been talking about the problem of wandering affections, where feelings have been aroused but no real sin committed. What happens, however, when a person allows their feelings to get the better of them and enters into sin? Sin can be committed in two ways—by thought and by deed. A person does not have to join themselves physically to a member of the opposite sex in order to commit adultery. According to Jesus it can be committed in the heart (Matthew 5:28).

Let me pause here to make clear the difference between a thought suddenly flashing into the mind and one that the mind steadily focuses upon. There is little one can do to control the thoughts that suddenly flash into the mind, but there is a great deal one can do to see that those thoughts are not entertained. If a thought enters a man's mind in which he sees himself in bed with a woman other than his wife, that thought, in itself, is not a sin. But if he focuses on that thought, entertains it in his mind, indulges in it and plays with it in his imagination, then he commits sin.

Dr W. E. Sangster described the process of temptation like this:

> A sinful thought comes and knocks on the door of the heart, but it brings a blush to the cheek and the door is slammed against it. But it comes again and again, gets fingered and looked at from other angles and is briefly considered . . . and then entertained; slowly it gets inside . . . until the sin is done. No blush now, no slammed door. The thought that once crimsoned your cheek stalks into your mind and takes its ease like a familiar visitor or an old friend.

Learn to recognize the difference between a thought that knocks at the door and one that is admitted and entertained. If an adulterous thought has been 'entertained', and the imagination has been used to conjure up a sexual act with another person other than your partner, then this must be repented of without delay. Repentance means telling God you are sorry for your sin, and not just for the sin but for the self-centredness that prompted it. The root of all sin is selfishness. It is wanting to have your own way even when your own way is diametrically opposed to God's way. And unless you repent of *that*—the desire to want your own way—then you have not really repented. It is not enough to lop off the branches—the axe must be applied to the root of the tree.

Listen to what James says about the act of repentance: 'God resisteth the proud, but giveth grace to the humble. Be humble then before God. But resist the devil and you'll find he'll run away from you. Come close to God and he will come close to you. You are sinners: get your hands clean again. Your loyalty is divided: get your hearts made true once more.... You should be deeply sorry, you should be grieved, you should even be in tears. Your laughter will have to become mourning, your high spirits will have to become dejection. You must humble yourselves in the sight of the Lord before he will lift you up' (James 4:6–10 PHILLIPS).

What if adultery has been committed, not just in thought but in deed? What are the steps a Christian should take in dealing with this serious problem? The same thing applies to an act of adultery committed in deed as one committed in thought—it should be dealt with by genuine repentance. When God's forgiveness has been sought and received, the person concerned should then contact the other person involved to ask them for their forgiveness, and to let them know, if the association has been a continuing one, that the relationship must now be broken. In taking steps to clear one's conscience, it is important to ask the forgiveness of the other person involved in terms such as these: 'God has convicted me of my wrong towards himself and towards you. I have already asked his forgiveness and now I would like to ask for your forgiveness. Will you forgive me for the wrong I have done you?' It may be, of course, that at this point the other person might not wish to break the association and may say that there is nothing to forgive. Do not be put off by this. If the other person wants to continue the affair, or will not offer you their forgiveness, then make it clear that as far as you are concerned the matter is now over. You have done what you should do and there your responsibility ends.

Confessing the sin to your marriage partner

The question now arises: should an act of adultery be confessed to one's marital partner? There can be no categorical answer to this question. Something in me longs to come up with a decisive answer but, all things considered, this is not possible. My mind goes back, as I write, to the interview I had with Bob whom I mentioned earlier in this chapter. After I exhorted Bob to repent of his sin, a repentance which was deeply moving and accompanied by a great flood of tears, he said to me, 'How am I going to tell my wife about this? She is a perfectionist and whenever she feels she has fallen beneath her own standards, she becomes depressed. I can't imagine what will happen when I tell her that I have committed adultery. She may never get over the shock.' At this point I shared with Bob several guidelines concerning confession which I have worked out over the years and are based on a faithfulness to Scripture and a sensitivity to the feelings of another person. These guidelines are an honest attempt to bring balance between these two important things.

Confession should be shared only when you feel sure it will help and not hinder the marital relationship. If, after prayer and much thought, you feel that a confession to your partner would destroy rather than develop your marital relationship, then, in my judgement, it would be right to withhold it. Sometimes choosing not to confess is the most loving thing to do. I remember an occasion when a man, after sharing with me the fact that he had committed adultery, said, 'I'm going straight home to tell my wife.' I happened to know that his wife was a deeply insecure person and, in addition, was suffering from a serious and longstanding sickness, so I advised against it—at least for the moment. 'But I have to tell her in order to find relief,' he countered. 'You must first find relief by confessing your sin to God,' I said, 'and when you have done this, you will be in a much better position to evaluate whether or not to tell your wife.' I then read to him the words of David, King of Israel, after he had confessed to God his adulterous affair with Bathsheba: 'What happiness for those whose guilt has been forgiven! What joys when sins are covered over! What relief for those who have confessed their sins and God has cleared their record' (Psalm 32:1–2 TLB).

'You see,' I went on, 'the whole point of repentance is to bring God's healing and forgiveness into your heart. If you want to confess to your wife simply to find relief, then you are acting out of a wrong motivation. Confess your sin to God, right here and now, and then see what God will direct you to do.' The man took my advice and openly repented of his sin right there in the counselling room. After about an hour, which was punctuated by brief prayers and deep sobbing, I asked him how he felt. 'I feel as if God has taken a great sponge and cleaned out my soul,' he said, at the same time brushing aside the moisture from under his eyes. We then sat and discussed the question whether or not he should confess to his wife. 'I see your point now,' he said. 'Before I simply wanted to clear my conscience without any thought of the effect and impact it might make upon her, but now that I know I am forgiven by God, I realize that a confession at this time might be destructive rather than healing in its effect.'

Actually, this man did confess the act of adultery to his wife about a year later, when she had recovered from her illness and their relationship had been brought to a higher and more meaningful level. In this matter of whether or not one should confess to one's partner, these questions ought to be uppermost in one's mind:

> Is my confession prompted by a desire to rid myself of a burden, or is it because I have the best interests of my partner at heart?
> Will my confession bring healing and understanding, or will it damage and destroy?
> Do I want to be healed at the expense of my partner's suffering?

If, after thinking these questions through, you feel that a confession would clear the air and produce a more open and honest relationship for you *and your partner,* then it would be right to go ahead. But if you are unsure, then it might be better to wait.

Confession should be made at an appropriate time and in an appropriate place. When a marriage partner decides it is right to make an open confession of wrongdoing, the timing and place of such a confession are vitally important. It would be decidedly inappropriate, for example, for one partner to confess to adultery to the other while they are in the midst of a heated discussion. A friend of mine who is a Christian counsellor, and who stresses the importance of timing in the act of confession, says, 'If a couple are watching a television programme, for example, where the act of adultery is being portrayed, and one partner comments on the situation as being despicable, it would not be in the best interests of the marriage for the other, who has committed adultery, to say, "I have done that." Such a confession at that moment would be unhelpful because the other partner would be psychologically and spiritually unprepared for it.'

Let me share with you a letter from my files in which a man tells how he prepared his wife for the distressing revelation that he had been guilty of conducting an extra-marital affair.

I did as you suggested and prayed that God would help me to discern the right timing for the unfolding of my sin that I knew had to come. I know from experience that my wife is at her best psychologically and spiritually halfway between her periods, so I planned my confession for a Wednesday night at that time. I have always fancied myself as a bit of a cook, so I announced a few nights before that on Wednesday night I would cook her a meal fit for a queen. She laughed and said, 'What have I done to deserve that?' On the Wednesday afternoon I came home early from my work (my wife was out as she works part-time in a chemist's shop every afternoon) and, after spending some time in prayer, began to prepare the meal. As I got involved in the cooking, I kept saying to myself, 'O Lord, prepare her heart and strengthen her spirit so that the hurt will not go too deep.' I found myself breaking out in a cold sweat as I rehearsed what I was going to say.

When she came home and saw the table laid so beautifully and smelled the aroma of the meal filling the house, she came over to me and gave me a long, lingering kiss. It almost broke my heart. We sat down together to the meal, and after it was finished she said, 'That was the most wonderful meal I have ever enjoyed.' Then she went on, 'What has happened to you over these past few weeks. You seem to be a different man? I must confess I like it, but I'm intrigued as to what has produced such a wonderful change in you?' I knew instinctively this was the moment. With tears running down my face I blurted it out. I told her what I had done and how I had wronged her, and asked her forgiveness. It was all over in a few minutes. She went quite white in the face, and after putting her head in her hands, began to cry softly. I put my arm round her shoulders and was grateful that she did not push me away. At last, after what seemed like hours, she looked up at me and said, 'Is this really true?' I said, 'Yes—and I'm so terribly sorry.' She was silent for about half-an-hour and then she looked into my eyes and said, 'I forgive you.'

I must confess I never expected to be forgiven that easily. I thought there would have been some vented hostility, even some smashing of plates (this is the way it has been in the past when things have gone wrong) and in a way I think I could have coped with that much better. Her forgiveness shattered me, but yet I knew it was what I longed for, next to God's forgiveness, as the most precious thing in the world.

I have thought a lot about my wanting her to reproach me rather than forgive me, and I see now that inwardly I was still blaming her, saying to myself, 'If she had given me more time and attention, this might not have happened.' Her forgiveness put things into perspective for me and overpowered all my self-justification.

I still can't believe the way things have turned out. I feel the most privileged person in the world. Knowing my wife as I do I expected spite and spleen, but she has never referred to it since—and now it is well over three months since this happened. She found a reservoir of forgiveness I never knew she had. I know God has truly been at work in our lives.

One last word about confession, and that is that *it should be undertaken in the most thoughtful, loving and considerate terms*. When making a confession, try as much as possible to keep away from vivid or specific details. Confession should not be so intimate, so revealing, so painful that it tears the other person's soul into shreds. One woman I know approached her husband with a confession that went something like this: 'You know how unhappy we have been in the past, and you have never been able to satisfy me sexually, so I have been having an affair with — — . It is over now, but we have slept together about fifteen times, four or five times in the back of his car, the other occasions in a motel. I know I was wrong, but in a way you drove me to it, but anyway I'm sorry.' A good example of how not to confess.

Here are some rules of thumb to follow when actually making a confession:

Rehearse carefully what you are going to say. Remember again the story of the prodigal son. He thought out his approach carefully beforehand: 'I will arise and go to my father, and will say...' (Luke 15:18).

Use words wisely. Words are powerful things. They can build up or they can tear down. If you say, 'We had intercourse together,' it will conjure up for your partner a picture of you making love to another person. It's better to say, 'We committed adultery.' That puts it in its proper perspective.

As far as possible, keep away from specific details. There is little point in mentioning how many times you were involved in an adulterous act, where it happened, or what procedures were adopted. Even if your partner asks for them, explain that because they are sinful memories they are best not recaptured.

Focus as much as possible on identifying the basic attitudes underlying the offence. Instead of saying, 'I'm sorry for the fact that I took — — to a hotel room and had intercourse,' say, 'I am sorry for my adultery and for my disloyalty to you.' Confessing basic attitudes gets to the root of the problem. The real offence is not just becoming involved in an extra-marital affair. The real sin is disloyalty, selfishness, self-centredness. Focus on the root cause and ask forgiveness for that.

Be on your guard for pride when making a confession. It's amazing how pride comes to our aid whenever we expose our sins and weaknesses so that we 'don't make fools of ourselves'. This inward pride reflects itself in such ways as these: we say, 'I have been wrong, but then you have been wrong too.' Or, 'I'm sorry, but you drove me to it.' Or, 'If I've been wrong about this, please forgive me.' The correct way of making a confession is to trample on pride, accept full responsibility for your actions and ask your partner's forgiveness in these words: 'I realize how wrong I have been in my selfishness and my disloyalty to you. Will you forgive me?' The words, 'Will you forgive me?' call for a definite response, and you encourage the other person to offer their forgiveness, thereby clearing the problem.

The offended partner

Let me now say a word to the offended partner in an extra-marital affair. What should you do, and how should you react when you discover that your partner has been unfaithful? The first emotion that will probably arise in your heart is that of anger. Anger at your partner, anger at the other person, and anger at yourself for letting yourself be deceived. I would encourage you to admit the anger, and let it surface in your heart. Some Christians have a tendency to pretend they are not angry. A woman I once counselled, whose husband had just confessed to an adulterous affair, tried to convince herself that she wasn't angry. When I said, 'Well, I would certainly be angry if that happened to me,' she said, 'But Christians are not supposed to get angry. It's an unbiblical way to behave.' I pointed out that there is a great difference between acknowledging one's anger and expressing it. It may be wrong sometimes to *express* anger but not wrong to feel it. As she permitted herself to feel her anger, she found a good deal of emotional release.

Accept responsibility for your anger by telling your partner, 'I feel angry,' or, 'I am deeply hurt,' rather than saying, 'You have made me angry,' or, 'You have hurt me deeply.' It is right to let your partner know your precise feelings, but it must be done in a way that does not project blame. Yes of course your partner is to blame, but it is not your responsibility to be your partner's judge. God is the judge: 'Vengeance is mine; I will repay, saith the Lord'

(Romans 12:19). If your partner has to go through some heavy discipline in their life, then let the Lord handle it. So say what you have to say once—and let it go.

Ask yourself some searching questions such as, 'Did I contribute in any way to my partner's downfall?' 'Is there some lack in me that I need to face and seek to develop?' The tendency here is to either blame yourself completely or to deny that you were to blame in any way. It's easy to go to extremes, especially when you are the victim of such shattering news; but try to be objective. It is easier said than done, I know, when your emotions are in an upheaval, but try anyway. If you can be objective enough at least to see the possibility of this, it can make a profound impression on your partner.

David Mace, in his book *Success in Marriage,* referring to a couple by the name of Jim and Alice, points out Jim's reaction to his wife's objectivity when confronted by his adultery. 'I'll never forget,' said Jim, 'how Alice behaved when my sordid little affair with the girl at the office blew up in her face. I knew it must be hurting her terribly—but she didn't whine and lash out. She sat down, looked me straight in the eye, and asked me where she had gone wrong, and what this girl had that she hadn't. In that moment I knew what a fine person Alice really was, and I felt ashamed of the whole business. From that moment the other girl didn't have a chance.'

Finally, forgive. I have outlined the principles of forgiveness in another chapter so I don't want to go over old ground here. Let Henry Ward Beecher have the last word on this subject:

'I can forgive but I cannot forget' is only another way of saying, 'I will not forgive.' Forgiveness ought to be like a cancelled note—torn in two and burned up, so that it can never be shown against anyone.

8

THANK GOD FOR SEX!

Fred and Fiona, married five years, had what their friends considered a happy marriage. And until they attended a seminar I conducted on the subject of *Family Life*, Fred and Fiona thought so too! A couple of statements I had made in the seminar sparked off a discussion between them that led, in turn, to the surfacing of several repressed fears and anxieties which they found deeply disturbing.

The statements I made which provoked them and led to them coming to me for counselling were these: 'Be open and honest with each other and share your feelings—both positive and negative—in an atmosphere of honesty and love,' and 'Thank God for sex.'

After the seminar had concluded, that night Fred shared with Fiona his honest feelings about their sexual relationship. 'I feel it can be greatly improved,' he said. 'I must admit I am becoming increasingly frustrated by your apparent coldness and frigidity.' At first Fiona was deeply upset by Fred's openness because, as she said to me in the first counselling session we had together, 'I never realized we had a problem until he shared it with me in that way.' I replied, 'You can be thankful he did, for many marriages get shipwrecked on the rocks of silence. If Fred hadn't shared with you in the way he did, he would have carried this in his heart perhaps for many years, and it would have soured your relationship without you really understanding why.'

But Fiona's biggest problem was with the statement I had made at the seminar, 'Thank God for sex.' Brought up in a home where the word 'sex' was never mentioned, she had come to believe that a physical relationship in marriage was something to be endured rather than enjoyed. 'I can't honestly thank God for sex,' she said, 'because sex for me is something God frowns upon.' Thankfully in the weeks that followed many of Fiona's mistaken ideas of the sexual relationship in marriage were put right, and in the last counselling session I had with Fred and Fiona they expressed their deep gratitude for the insights I had shared, which, they said, had brought a joy into their sexual relationship that had never been there—even in the first few months of their marriage.

In all the years I have been counselling Christian couples, I never cease to be amazed at the strange ideas some have on the subject of sex. In spite of the clear teaching of the Bible, many think that sex and holiness are antithetical, that sex and the Christian faith do not mix. One woman told me once that, for her, sex is something to be practised in the dark 'when God is not looking'. The Christian church has suffered from many unbiblical conclusions concerning sex. Happily these are in the process of correction.

One of the early church fathers by the name of Origen said, 'Adam did not have sexual knowledge of his wife until after the fall. If it had not been for the fall, the human race would very likely have been propagated in some mysterious or angelic manner without sex and, therefore, sin.' Jerome, another early Christian teacher, said, 'It is good for a man not to touch a woman. It is evil to do so. [Note the false move of logic.] Marriage cannot be good because it makes prayer difficult. Those individuals who have become saints even though they were married, did so because they remained virgins even in marriage.'

During the Middle Ages, we are told, the church went to great extremes to downgrade the sexual relationship in marriage. Dwight Small in his book, *Christian, Celebrate Your Sexuality* (Fleming H. Revell 1974), stated, 'Complete abstinence from sex relationships had to be maintained on no less than five days out of seven. On Thursdays in memory of the arrest of our Lord, on Fridays in honour of his death, on Saturdays in honour of the virgin Mary, on Sundays in honour of the resurrection, and on Mondays in honour of the faithful departed.' That left just two days in which married couples could enjoy a sexual relationship. Aren't you glad you didn't live in such restricted times?

However, even today, unhealthy attitudes towards sex still persist in some Christians' minds. But sex is God's idea! He thought it up in the beginning. In fact the very first thing God draws attention to, following the creation of Adam and Eve, is their sexuality: 'male and female created he them' (Genesis 1:27). Let me share with you now some of the suggestions I shared with Fred and Fiona on the subject of sex, and which I have also shared with thousands of others in counselling and seminar sessions. These suggestions, I need hardly say, are intended to be used inside marriage, for I regard sexual experience outside of marriage in the same way that the Bible does—as sin.

Educate yourself in basic sexual matters

Every man and woman should have a basic knowledge of the male and female anatomy. 'God has never put a premium on ignorance,' says Tim LaHaye, 'and that includes sex education.' Even in this enlightened age when there are so many Christian books on the subject of sex, I still come across Christian couples who know little about the reproductive organs and sexual functions.

Tim, a 30-year-old accountant, was like this. He came to me for counselling, following a seminar session in which I had said: 'There is one point in a woman's body to which a man ought to pay attention when preparing to make love to his wife—the clitoris.' 'Can you tell me where the clitoris is?' he said, 'because I don't have the slightest idea myself.' I took out a diagram of the female anatomy which I keep for sexual counselling and showed him. I have to admit that I find it unbelievable that so many men don't take the trouble to find out some of the most basic things which make the difference between a happy and unhappy sexual relationship in marriage.

Women, too, need to acquaint themselves with the male anatomy, especially the reproductive organs. But let's face it—one doesn't really need to read a book to discover that. God didn't give Adam and Eve a manual on sexual behaviour; they learned by doing. I am convinced that, if a man and woman set out in their sexual relationship *to bring pleasure to the other partner rather than gain pleasure for themselves,* it will bring their love-making into a new and thrilling dimension.

Pay attention to the emotional and sexual differences which exist between men and women

'I'm convinced,' says one writer, 'that the average male could probably have sex and reach a climax right in the middle of a bitter argument with his wife, or even while watching television.' To a man, when the sexual urge strikes him, the mood and surrounding circumstances make little difference. Men tend to isolate sex from other emotions by placing it in one of life's 'compartments'. There is a time to work, a time to eat, a time to read one's Bible, a time to pray, and a time for sex.

But for a woman sex is of a different order. She sees sex

in a far wider setting than the bedroom—she sees it in the total setting of her relationship with her husband in every aspect of her marriage.

'I wish you'd begin making love to me during the day, even at breakfast,' said one woman to her husband in a fit of anger. 'Then perhaps I'd be a little more passionate at bedtime.' What did she mean? She was trying to tell her husband that, for her, sexual arousal does not begin in the bedroom. It may end there, but it begins in an atmosphere of love and tenderness *hours* before a sexual encounter is experienced. While a husband may be able to move straight from an argument into sexual intimacy, a wife needs to be courted and wooed. Successful sex, to her, is more than just the experience of an orgasm—it is the entire setting of intimacy surrounding her marriage. A man tends to believe that a good physical relationship is necessary for a good all-round relationship, but a woman believes and thinks differently. She believes that a good all-round relationship is the proper basis on which to build a physical one.

Oliver, an elder in a church I once pastored, confided in me one day that the sexual side of his marriage was dull and unexciting. 'Whenever I watch my wife undress,' he said, 'I am ready for sex immediately, but however hard I try to arouse or stimulate my wife, she seems to show no interest.' My advice to Oliver was similar to the advice I have given to many other men in this position: 'Prepare your wife for love-making not in the bedroom but in the living room. You see,' I went on, 'whilst a man is turned on sexually by what he sees, a woman is stimulated more by what she hears. This means that to have an enjoyable sex life, don't just wait until your wife gets into the bedroom before you tell her that you love her. Say it in the living room, because the setting and the mood from which a sexual union is initiated is crucial to her.'

Oliver did as I suggested, and although at first his wife

was a little suspicious, she came to enjoy her husband's loving and romantic attentions. Even though this incident took place twelve years ago I still remember the twinkle in Oliver's eye when he told me one day, 'It used to be me that couldn't wait to get into the bedroom at night—not any more!'

In counselling women over the years and listening to their deep concerns in many hours of interview sessions, I have come to recognize that women have a basic fear reverberating deep inside them—*the fear of being treated as an object and not as a person*. 'All my husband wants,' they say, 'is sex—and when that is over he shows no further interest in me.' When a man steps out of his own self-concern and unselfishly focuses on understanding his wife's needs and ministers to them, he never loses, but always gains. The same is true for the wife. When she seeks to understand the differences between her and her husband and adjusts to them, she too will enrich her relationship with her husband and add a new dimension to her marriage.

I said earlier that a man is turned on sexually by what he sees. A wife who recognizes this and wants to please her husband will overcome any inhibitions she may have about undressing in front of him. And at times, if for his sake and not for her own sake, she will allow him to make love to her... with the light on!

Concentrate on developing a good technique in foreplay

It has been said that there is no such thing as a frigid woman—only a clumsy man. This is a generalization, of course, but there are a tragic number of marriages today that bear out that statement. Selfishness and ignorance on the part of the husband can drive a woman to literal aversion to sexual contact. The all-important word in foreplay is *tenderness*. If agape love (i.e. love which finds as much pleasure in giving as receiving) does not rule your heart, then sex will never rise higher than the sensual.

A good model of foreplay is provided for us in the Scriptures: 'His left hand is under my head,' says the woman in the Song of Solomon, 'and with his right hand he embraces me' (Song of Solomon 2:6 TLB). Here the husband is apparently lying on his side, next to his wife with his left arm under her head where he can easily fondle her with his right hand. Women vary in the amount of satisfaction they derive from stimulation of the breasts, but research suggests that most women get great pleasure from this experience.

How long a couple spend in foreplay varies with each couple's needs, but it is never wise to be in a hurry. There is no universal pattern for arousing a woman to love-making. The important thing is to know what pleases your wife in sexual stimulation—*and do it*. She will have her own little secrets as to what best prepares her for fulfilment. This is why it is important to know the person—not just the method.

Intimate verbal communication should never cease during foreplay. Assure your wife that you love her and that she means everything to you. Take a tip from Solomon who knew how to make his beloved happy. He uses lots of endearing words and, as we say, 'sweet nothings'. One final tip for husbands—cut your nails. Keeping your nails trimmed and clean is essential for those intimate moments. A ragged nail in foreplay can affect your wife's sex drive in the same way that an ice-cold shower affects yours!

The question is often asked me, when counselling married couples, 'What about oral sex? Is this permissible for Christians?' I hold the view, along with most other Christian counsellors, that providing *both* husband and wife are happy about it and it does not become a substitute for intercourse, then I would not personally regard it as wrong. Some women are repelled by the suggestion of oral sex, and if this is so then a husband should be willing to sacrifice his own desires in this matter out of consideration for his wife. Abnormal behaviour such as cruelty, anal intercourse, or practices suggested by the pornographers will be repugnant to Christians who have taken the trouble to develop a sensitive conscience. Nothing should ever be forced on one partner by another.

And now a word to the women. Remember, no man can become a great lover without a responsive woman. Make up your mind to give yourself to your husband in joyful abandonment. Help him to know what he is doing right by complimenting him. And when he is doing something wrong, tell him—but tell him *gently*.

Face sexual problems with hope

There are three main problems encountered by married couples in relation to this matter of sex. They are as follows: inability to come to an orgasm, premature ejaculation, and impotence. The first relates to the woman, the others to the man.

It is estimated that 30–40% of women have difficulty in reaching an orgasm. Sometimes women say, 'I'm not sure if I have ever had an orgasm or not. I enjoy sex but I've never felt an intense, overwhelming feeling such as some books describe.' Others state: 'I feel greatly aroused, but my feelings never overflow.' A small number of women fake a sexual climax in order not to give their husbands a feeling of inadequacy.

One reason why a woman fails to achieve an orgasm is due to inadequate foreplay. Physical foreplay by the husband should last anywhere from ten to twenty minutes—sometimes longer. Another reason can be the repressed fears and anxieties of childhood. For example, if a girl did not have a close and loving relationship with her father, this can result in an inability to feel 'really close' to her husband. Yet another reason for a failure to achieve an orgasm can be a woman's negative self-image. She may see herself as unworthy of love, and this negative self-concept can dampen, to some extent, her emotional and physical reactions.

Most orgasmic problems can be overcome by the husband giving more care and consideration to the matter of foreplay. If the orgasmic difficulty is rooted in the repressed problems of childhood, then counselling ought to be sought. Another way to overcome orgasmic difficulty is that suggested by Dr Arnold H. Kegel, a specialist in female disorders. He claims that when treating patients with problems of incontinence, he discovered that by encouraging them to exercise the puboccygeus muscle, which is at the base of the pelvis, some women found in consequence that, whereas before they were unable to achieve a sexual climax with their husbands, they were now able to do so. Though Kegel's primary interest has not been in sexual problems, he felt obliged to pursue the sexual component of his findings. As a result he has helped many women, through proper exercise, to achieve increased sexual enjoyment. For more detailed information on this subject, see the chapter 'A Key to Feminine Response' in the book *The Act of Marriage* by Tim and Beverly LaHaye (Zondervan).

The second problem usually encountered in the sexual area of marriage is that of premature ejaculation. This happens when a man is unable to control the timing of his ejaculation, and reaches a climax either before intercourse or immediately upon entering his wife. Men usually feel very embarrassed about this problem, but it can be overcome with a little understanding and some patience. One way is for the man to focus his thoughts during foreplay on things that have nothing to do with sex at all. This is a common but not always effective strategy for keeping arousal at pre-ejaculation level. A better way of overcoming the problem is the method advocated by Masters and Johnson, two sex therapists who have conducted an intensive research into sexual problems. They suggest that the wife and husband practise for some weeks what they call 'squeezing exercises'. The husband, whenever he feels himself about to have a climax, indicates this to his wife and she, in turn, squeezes the top of his penis with her finger and thumb, a practice which helps to stop ejaculation and cause sexual tension to subside. Couples have told me that after several weeks of practising this method, it has completely solved the husband's problem of premature ejaculation.

The third sexual problem encountered in marriage is that of impotence. Impotence is an inability to achieve an erection or to sustain a sufficient erection to have intercourse. Men feel about impotence the way women feel about an inability to achieve an orgasm—frustrated. All sexual difficulties involve two things: (1) relationship problems; and (2) technique problems. In my experience, impotence usually arises from fatigue, depression, hostility, guilt, or the result of long years of continued masturbation.

Basic to the problem of impotency is that of *anxiety*. To overcome this problem one must approach the object of anxiety, which is intercourse, with gentleness and sensitivity. The main problem is the pressure to perform, and here the wife can contribute greatly. She must make it clear that she loves her husband whether he performs or not. A modern approach to the treatment of impotency (and this is purely a technique solution rather than a relationship one) is to encourage husband and wife to lie together in bed, naked, and embrace each other. They are specifically instructed *not* to attempt intercourse no matter how erect the man becomes, nor how much the wife wants to complete the act. Pressure is thus removed while expectation of erection is enhanced. This is kept up for a week or so, and the results are quite astonishing. Once the pressure to perform has been taken away from the man, he more often than not finds an inner release that enables him to move towards a happy and joyous sexual relationship with his wife.

Cultivate cleanliness

'The best sex aids ever invented,' said a Christian wife, 'are soap, toothpaste and deodorant.' Men need to pay particular attention to this matter, as women have a delicate sense of smell that is far more sensitive than men's. Have you ever noticed your wife going through the house saying, 'What's that smell?' and you replied, '*What* smell?' Whenever I open the door of our refrigerator, and inside there is something 'going off', my wife can smell it even though she may be in another room. I can't smell it even if it is sitting on my upper lip!

'A woman's acute sense of smell, together with her innate desire for cleanliness,' says one male writer, 'can detect an all-day armpit long before we even begin to make our move.' One woman once said to me, 'My husband spends half an hour preparing himself to go to work in the morning, but he won't spend five minutes preparing himself to be at his best when we go to bed and have sex.'

Then what about bad breath? A couple I counselled recently told me that their sexual relationship had dwindled to the act of intercourse taking place no more than once every three months. I could find no answer to their situation until in one session I commented on the man's bad breath. I hadn't raised it earlier because I thought he might be having some temporary difficulties, but each time I talked to him it had grown worse. His breath could have knocked out Muhammed Ali in a single second!

When I commented on this, gently and sensitively, I

saw an expression on his wife's face that I hadn't seen
before, so I pursued the matter with her for a few minutes.
'Do you find this a problem when you are in bed together?'
I asked. She didn't answer for a full five minutes and then
said, 'I don't think that I could ever have mentioned it
unless I was forced to, but yes, it is a problem. In fact, I
think it is the root cause of all our troubles.' I encouraged
the man to pay a visit to his dentist to locate the source of
the trouble. It was a bad tooth. When it was removed, his
wife said it was like being married all over again. 'I could
never have believed,' she said, 'that a little thing like that
could get to me—but it did!' So, remember, if your wife
swoons whenever you approach her, it might not be due
to your romantic vibes! Perhaps she is trying to give you a
hint.

Make sex an act of worship

It is only in recent years that marriage counsellors have
become concerned with encouraging couples to aim for a
far deeper intimacy than that of the joining of their bodies.
The problem is illustrated in an article entitled 'How Good
is Your Marriage?' (*This Week* magazine, USA):

Tearfully...an attractive woman told her best friend that her
nineteen-year-old marriage was over. None of the standard
problems—sex, money, children—had ever troubled them.
But, nevertheless, a gulf had slowly opened between her and
her husband. Why? They had failed to meet marriage's
deepest, most subtle test—the challenge of intimacy.

Intimacy for most people has become synonymous with
sex. But for the modern psychiatrists and marriage counsellors, the word far transcends the sexual. Intimacy is not an
act; it is a state of existence in which two people gradually
share more and more of their innermost thoughts and experiences. This continuing growth is the key to a loving relationship.

Intimacy...between a married couple must involve total personality contact....

A total personality contact is more than the joining of two human bodies. It is more than the joining of two human souls—mind, emotions and will. It takes place only when the physical and psychological parts of our being are complemented by the spiritual. This is something that is absolutely amazing and wonderful. It makes sex an act of worship. The sexual act is one of the most beautiful experiences in the world. During the sexual act, two Christians can enjoy themselves, and the openness they reveal to each other can result in a new openness to God. They are given the greatest opportunity not only to understand themselves but also their partner, and that results in their relating more closely to God.

Sex is not dirty; it can become an act of worship. We are doing what God designed us to do. We achieve total oneness and union. The prolonged, controlled and lovingly executed act of sex is God's way of demonstrating to us the great spiritual truth of how intimately Jesus Christ is related to us and loves the church. Some Christians relax and praise the Lord, thanking him for the intimacy of the love they have shared. It is more for Christians than the joining of their bodies; it is the joining of their spirits. It is true that some Christians see it as sordid, and suffer from inhibitions and ideas concerning sex; but seen in its proper light and within the bounds of marriage, it is one of life's most pleasurable and beautiful experiences.

9

REMEMBER YOUR PROMISES

'"For better, for worse...for richer, for poorer...in sickness and in health...till death us do part." When he said those words in church five years ago, I thought he meant them and that nothing would ever come between us...but last night he told me that he wanted a divorce.'

Betty, a twenty-five-year-old wife and mother, sat opposite me in the counselling room, desperately trying to hold back her tears as she recounted the conversation between herself and her husband, George, the night before. 'When we made those vows,' she went on, 'we made them as fully committed Christians, and I would never have dreamt that our problems would finally lead to the possibility of our marriage being dissolved. What shall I do? Please help me.'

I encouraged Betty to share with me some of the details surrounding the problem; not only to provide me with the salient facts, but also to give her an opportunity to air her feelings and release some of the emotional pressure that was building up inside her.

Betty and George's problems began, it seems, almost as soon as their honeymoon was over. At first it was little disagreements, but over the months, the 'little disagreements' grew into big giants. Several times Betty had suggested seeing a Christian counsellor, but George's usual reply was, 'What can a counsellor do? If you weren't so stubborn we wouldn't have any serious problems. Why waste the time of a counsellor when he can only tell you what you already know?'

For almost an hour I listened to Betty's story as she surveyed the past five years of her married life—an hour that was punctuated with long pauses and deep sighs. 'George thinks our basic problem is that we are incompatible,' she said. 'If that is so, then I don't suppose it's worth trying to do anything to save our marriage. Do you agree?'

'Incompatibility is not a reason for divorce,' I said. 'That's the reason for marriage.' Betty's eyes opened wide at that remark. It's not the first time I have seen someone react in surprise when that fact is presented. 'What do you mean?' said Betty. 'I've never heard anyone say that before.'

'Well, you see,' I went on, 'God wants us to have a lifetime of opportunity in which we can develop our characters, learn the principles of genuine love, overcome irritation, practise the art of forgiving, adapt, serve, grow together...and where better than marriage for that to be accomplished?'

'Do you really mean there is a possibility that George and I can make it together?' asked Betty.

'I don't see why not,' I replied. 'Thousands of others have found that a marriage breakdown can become a marriage breakthrough—and so can you. Now let's set up a few appointments for you and George, and with God's help you can start rebuilding your marriage according to his pattern in the Scriptures.'

Fortunately, George was fully co-operative in undergoing some in-depth marriage counselling, and after a few months of acquainting them with the biblical principles of conflict resolution, communication and building family unity, they began to move towards a more secure and meaningful relationship.

Betty and George's marriage is by no means an isolated case. Almost every day I hear of a Christian couple who have either separated or are seeking a divorce. And to me this is one of the most alarming trends in the Christian church today. 'Christians once watched the climbing divorce rate with smugness,' says Gerald L. Dahl, 'but now the epidemic of marital failure has reached them.'

Divorce is not a solution. After years of working with Christians facing serious marital problems, I am beginning to understand God's powerful response to Israel: 'I hate divorce' (Malachi 2:16, NIV).

We live in a strange society which has some strange notions. The media present divorce as something quite commonplace. One writer says:

> Suppose you and I were treated in hospital the way divorce is treated on television. We'd die! Imagine, for instance, being in an accident, rushed to the hospital and carted into an emergency ward all battered up. A man walks in who calls himself a doctor and says, 'This is a mess. For all practical purposes the patient is dead already. There are probably lots of hidden pressures building up also, causing other complications. He's beyond mending. Let's walk away from this, turn out the lights and go home.' Ridiculous? Not at all when you consider that some counsellors are actually *paid* for prescribing divorce as the answer for a troubled marriage.

Whenever a couple approach me for advice on the subject of divorce, I do everything in my power to persuade them differently. I say to them, 'You promised God and each other that you would stay married for the rest of your life. Now let me help show you how it can be done.' God often allows marital pressures to build up in order to cause the persons concerned to seek his solution and develop an understanding of biblical principles.

It is my belief that the Christian church is contributing

to the break-up of many marriages by its failure to provide good marriage-guidance counselling based on the principles of the word of God. Time and time again, couples tell me, 'There isn't anyone in our church who can talk to us. Our minister is far too busy and no one else seems to have the understanding or concern to help us with our marriage problems.' It is time the church woke up to its responsibilities and tackled this problem head-on. Today there is hardly a church without someone in its congregation having experienced the pain of divorce. But the tragic thing is that many Christians have come to accept divorce as the only option in a troubled marriage. Is this because we are slowly being brain-washed by the world into accepting standards that are below the level of the Scriptures?

When I entered the Christian ministry, now well over thirty years ago, I thought my views on the subject of divorce were clearly set. I regarded divorce as a non-option. Later, when I met heartbreaking cases in the churches I pastored and in counselling sessions I conducted, I felt that the Scriptures ought to be balanced by a more compassionate view. I said to myself: 'Concentrating my attention on the passages that speak of divorce hinders me from seeing the wider application of the Christian message to the problem of divorce. A strictly exegetical interpretation of the divorce passages is not the way to arrive at a balanced assessment of truth.'

So in the interests of compassion, I somewhat modified my views and came to regard divorce, in some circumstances, as permissible. Several years ago, however, I became greatly troubled by my position, and in order to settle the matter in my mind once and for all, I decided to refrain from giving any advice on the subject of divorce for a whole year, during which time I researched the subject once again, as thoroughly and as painstakingly as possible. I came to see that the Scriptures speak to the issue of divorce with great clarity, and that true compassion comes not from focusing on the heartbreaking problems that some couples encounter in their marriage, but from aligning oneself with God's standards and solutions.

Time and time again I have heard people say, 'But we must have compassion in our interpretation of the Scriptures relating to divorce.' This raises the question: do we arrive at truth through our feelings or through spiritual discernment? Rarely am I accused of lack of compassion. Those I have counselled over the years have witnessed me weep with them in their troubles. My heart overflows with care and concern for those who have hit serious problems in their marriages, but I have come to the conclusion that *real* care and concern consists in helping couples see God's answers to their problems.

Divorce is not a popular subject. Many ministers have told me that they are reluctant to offer biblical teaching on the subject of divorce because they do not want to offend those already divorced and remarried. Let me share with you now what I consider to be the biblical view on this vital question of divorce and remarriage.

Broadly speaking, the views of most evangelical Christians fall into the following three categories:

1. Those who believe that divorce and remarriage is never justified and that marriage is indissoluble until the death of one of the partners.

2. Those who believe that divorce and remarriage is permissible only for adultery and desertion.

3. Those who believe that divorce and remarriage may be tolerated when a marriage which begins with two non-Christians falls apart when one of them later becomes a Christian. If the non-Christian partner, for this reason, wants to end the marriage, the Christian is not to resist this action.

I subscribe to the first of the above views. I believe a

marriage commitment, made between two persons of opposite sex and physically consummated, is indissoluble until the death of one of the partners.

What is marriage?

The question of divorce and remarriage cannot be seen in its proper perspective until we determine what exactly is a marriage. In Bible times, marriage was not a specifically religious ceremony. Even in Christ's day, there was no legal registration of marriage, neither was it accompanied by a religious service or ceremony. This was because the whole of life was deemed to be 'religious'. God has handed over to society the responsibility for supervising and upholding the sacred bond of marriage, and the guidelines God gave to society are to be found in a simple but concise statement made by the Almighty in the Garden of Eden and recorded for us in Genesis 2:24: 'Therefore shall a man leave his father and his mother, and shall cleave unto his wife: and they shall be one flesh.' This, by the way, is the only statement about marriage which is repeated on four other occasions in the Bible—in the same form and language—Matthew 19:5, Mark 10:7, 1 Corinthians 6:16 and Ephesians 5:31. Marriage, according to this statement, consists of three steps and stages; and although I have listed these three steps elsewhere in this book, I feel it necessary to review them once again here:

1. *Leaving:* moving away from the emotional ties of a father/mother relationship.

2. *Cleaving:* entering into a new husband/wife relationship.

3. *One flesh:* consummating the new union by the act of sexual intercourse.

Society has been given the responsibility by God to supervise and uphold the marriage commitment. It does so when it encourages two people about to enter into marriage to do so openly and publicly before the whole community, thus demonstrating two things: (1) they are no longer 'on the market', so to speak, and (2) they are making a lifelong commitment to each other in the presence of witnesses.

In my view a civil marriage is as valid as a religious marriage. The heart of the covenant of marriage, it should be remembered, is the agreement made between the two people involved. Some people speak of 'the minister who married us', but actually no minister married them—they married themselves. In Great Britain the only difference between a church wedding and one conducted in a registry office is that, in the case of the former, prayer is made and God's blessing is pronounced on the union by a minister.

It is, of course, good that a Christian couple make their commitment in church, surrounded by Christian traditions and ceremonies, but whether a couple get married in church or in a registry office, they are joined together in the sight of God, who is the source of all authority, both religious and secular (see Romans 13:1–6). God expects them to honour their covenant until the death of one of the partners dissolves the union. Those who say they were never joined together by God because they were married before becoming Christians are failing to comprehend the true nature of marriage. 'Therefore what God has joined together, let man not separate' (Matthew 19:6 NIV) applies to the whole of society.

Two puzzling scriptures

As most of the arguments concerning divorce and remarriage centre around two texts, I want to examine them with you now in some detail.

Marital unfaithfulness

The first is Matthew 19:9, 'I tell you that anyone who

divorces his wife, except for marital unfaithfulness, and
marries another woman commits adultery' (NIV). Those
who use this text to support the view that divorce is permissible on the grounds of marital unfaithfulness are not
only building a doctrine on one word but are also using a
wrong translation for the word. The original Greek word
used here in the text is *porneia* which cannot be restricted
to marital unfaithfulness. If Jesus really meant marital
unfaithfulness, he would have used the word *moichos*
which means adultery. Christ's use of the word *porneia* is
very important, because that word refers to immorality
during the Jewish betrothal period and discovered only
after marriage has taken place. We will never understand
or comprehend the meaning of this passage until we
understand the picture of engagement and marriage which
Jesus had in mind when he uttered these words.

A Jewish marriage consisted of the following sequences:

1. The prospective bridegroom took the initiative and
travelled from his father's house to the home of the prospective bride.

2. The father of the prospective bride then negotiated
with the prospective bridegroom the price that had to be
paid.

3. When the bridegroom paid the purchase price the
marriage covenant was then established. At this point,
the man and woman were regarded as married, even
though no physical union had taken place.

4. The covenant involved drinking from a cup over
which the betrothal benediction had been pronounced.
This symbolized a covenant relationship.

5. After the marriage covenant the groom left the house
of the bride and returned to his father's house.

6. During the waiting time until the actual moment of
marriage, the bride gathered her wardrobe and the groom
attended to the necessity of arranging accommodation for
himself and his bride.

7. At a pre-arranged time the groom accompanied by male escorts left the house of his father, usually after darkness had descended, and went in a torchlit procession to the home of the bride.

8. The bride, although knowing the approximate time of the groom's arrival, would not know the exact time, and would thus live in a state of constant anticipation. Thus the groom's arrival was always preceded by a shout.

9. The groom then went into the bride's house to receive his bride with her female attendants, and then returned with her to his father's house.

10. The bride and groom, upon returning to the father's house (or their own prepared living accommodation), would, in the privacy of that place, enter into physical union for the first time, thereby consummating the marriage.

(This outline of betrothal and marriage sequence was originally drawn up by Bill Gothard, an American Bible teacher, following study of customs and procedures in ancient Israel.)

Keeping in mind that the above was the picture Christ had of engagement and marriage, if the bride had been unfaithful between the time when the groom entered into the covenant and drank the cup and the time he took his bride to himself, the groom had a legal right to divorce her. This is the historical setting of the text we are looking at, and without an understanding of the background to this passage, a true interpretation cannot possibly be given.

The very situation which Joseph and Mary experienced during their engagement or betrothal period is an example of the true meaning of what is sometimes called 'the exception clause'. While Joseph and Mary were still engaged, and before they had physically consummated their marriage, Mary was found to be with child of the Holy Spirit. Because Joseph loved Mary and did not want to make her a public example, he considered quietly divorcing her (Matthew 1:18–20).

Before leaving this passage, let's look at it in another light. The Pharisees asked Jesus, 'Is it lawful for a man to divorce his wife for any and every reason?' (Matthew 19:3 NIV). Christ's answer is extremely significant. Instead of allowing himself to be entangled in a number of arguments which the Pharisees would be able to bring up from the law of Moses, he went back to God's original design for marriage, 'Haven't you read...that at the beginning the Creator "made them male and female", and said, "For this reason a man will leave his father and mother and be united to his wife, and the two will become one flesh"?... Therefore what God has joined together, let man not separate' (Matthew 19:4–6 NIV).

Had the Pharisees really been seeking to do God's will, they would have accepted the words of Jesus here without any further argument. But being argumentative and seeking to use the Scriptures to justify their preconceived ideas, they went on, 'Why then...did Moses command that a man give his wife a certificate of divorce?' (Matthew 19:7 NIV). The obvious aim of the Pharisees was to use the Old Testament to justify divorce and remarriage; whereas Jesus used the Old Testament to emphasize the permanency of marriage.

Christ's answer to the Pharisees is applicable to those today who—instead of coming to the Bible for light on the subject of divorce and remarriage determined to do God's will whatever the cost—come looking for scriptural reasons to support their preconceived ideas. This is what the Master said: 'Moses permitted you to divorce your wives because your hearts were hard. But it was not this way from the beginning' (Matthew 19:8 NIV).

If the Pharisees had really been wanting to do God's will, they would have accepted Christ's words without equivocation. The Master went right back to the original creation and re-emphasized God's order. God made no provision for divorce when he instituted marriage in the beginning (Genesis 2:23–24).

If we come to the Bible looking for ways by which we can justify divorce and remarriage, we are no better than the Pharisees of Jesus' day. It is perfectly true that Moses allowed divorce because of their 'hardness of heart', but we who are Christ's people must ask ourselves: do we want to be guilty of having our own way over this issue out of hardness of heart, or do we want to follow God's commands which emphasize the permanency of marriage?

To sum up: the exception clause referred to earlier relates to betrothal unfaithfulness. If a man found that his wife was not a virgin when he married her, he was given an option in Deuteronomy 22:13–21 of divorcing her. This is the situation illustrated in Matthew 1:19. The reason why the exception clause is not recorded in the other gospels is because Matthew was writing to Jewish readers who would understand the unique betrothal customs to which it referred.

This definition does not allow the notion that sexual intercourse before marriage establishes a marriage union. Sexual union after the ceremony of marriage consummates it, but sexual union before it does not establish it. Likewise, this definition does not allow for adultery or fornication dissolving it. Sin does not have the capacity to destroy what God has created.

A non-Christian partner

Now let's turn to the second text around which argument revolves concerning divorce and remarriage. 'But if the unbeliever leaves, let him do so. A believing man or woman is not bound in such circumstances; God has called us to live in peace' (1 Corinthians 7:15 NIV). What does it mean when it says, 'A believing man or woman is not bound in such circumstances'?

This passage deals with the subject of a Christian whose

unbelieving partner wants to leave the marriage because they do not want to live with a Christian partner. But Paul's words in verse 15 must not be construed to mean that he is encouraging remarriage. Remember the whole tenor of 1 Corinthians 7 is to encourage singleness, not remarriage (see verses 7, 8, 10, 11, 27, 32, 33, 34, 39 and 40). The phrase 'not bound in such circumstances' refers (in my view) to the law of the husband, not the law of God. When an unbelieving husband divorces his wife, she is no longer under his headship and is not expected to submit to his authority or succumb to his sexual advances. Sometimes divorced women have a conflict here, when after the divorce the ex-husband returns and makes sexual advances to his former wife. What is she to do? If she views her marriage as indissoluble, must she go along with his desires? Paul says no. She can rightfully refuse his overtures because she is no longer bound. Nevertheless, she must continue to obey the commands of God, which include not breaking her marriage vows by marrying another person.

When I shared these biblical views in a counselling session with a lady called Jean whose husband, a non-Christian, had divorced her, she became extremely agitated and said, 'Does this mean that I can never marry again? Surely God loves me too much to let me spend the rest of my days in singleness?'

I said, 'Jean, what you seem to be saying is, "No matter what God says, I still think I have a right to be remarried as I can't be expected to go through life in a single state." Now I can understand this feeling, but let me help you discover how the Lord can help you cope with the issue of singleness.' I then went on to explain that thousands of Christians are mistaken in their view of singleness. This is because they have never learned to delight themselves in the Lord *alone*.

One writer I know, a Christian psychologist, claims that

in order for a person to live happily in this world, they need nothing but the Lord and what he chooses to provide. 'Without noticing what is happening,' he says, 'believers drift away from absolute reliance on the Lord, and while continuing to assert the adequacy of Jesus, begin looking to others *rather than* to the Lord for satisfaction of their personal needs.'

When I put this point to Jean, her response was this: 'I can't argue with the fact that Christ can meet my personal needs, for I believe the Scripture which says that I am "complete in him" (Colossians 2:10), but what I can't face is the thought of no loving human arms around me, no physical touch, no face to look into. I know the Lord is within me, but how am I going to cope with the lack of a warm loving human being to comfort and caress me?'

I said, 'Jean, let me assure you I know exactly what you are saying. Though Christ can meet your needs, he is not a physical being—someone you can touch or can see. And that desire for physical companionship is not something I am ignoring. I recognize it is there and it is valid and real. What I am saying, however, is that when we learn to be content in Christ, and in him alone, then the effect it has upon us is not to isolate us from disappointment or from hurt, but that the hurt is assuaged by the reality of Christ's presence in such a way that the disappointment never becomes devastating.'

Jean was not convinced, but when I saw her several months later, she told me that although she had rejected what I had said, she had come to see that her situation had been a time in which she had gained a more intimate knowledge of the Lord, and that her Christian commitment had deepened to a great degree.

Believe me, I am not insensitive or unmindful of the hurt and sense of loss that a divorced person feels, but I would be failing to interpret Scripture right if I did not say that the hurts and heartaches that come our way, whether through a broken marriage or anything else, can, if properly understood and surrendered to God, draw a person closer to the Lord and bring them into a new awareness of his love.

'What if I have already remarried?'

There will be some reading these lines who are divorced and remarried and, being convinced of the truth of my interpretation of the Scriptures, might be saying to themselves: 'Since I am wrong in remarrying, ought I to leave my present partner?' My answer would be no. I base that reply on the principle found in Deuteronomy 24:4 where God expressly forbids a divorced woman who has remarried to return to her first husband—even if the second husband dies. One commentator believes (and it is a view with which I concur) that God established this principle for two main reasons: (1) switching marriage partners is devastating to society and to any children involved—it is better to stay in the present situation than to complicate the issue further, and perhaps bring greater hurt and confusion to any children from the second marriage; (2) God wants to use a binding relationship to overcome an independent or rebellious spirit.

Some time ago a couple read a leaflet I had produced in which I outlined my views on the subject of divorce and remarriage in the way I have done in these pages. Feeling that the arguments I had presented were incontrovertible (though not all would view them in this way), they wrote to me asking what position they now ought to adopt in their church and in society as they were both divorced and remarried. I encouraged them to do three things. The first was to repent and ask God's forgiveness for disobeying his word. Four times in Scripture God says that a man commits adultery when he marries a divorced woman whose husband is still living—Matthew 5:32; 19:9; Luke 16:18;

Romans 7:2–3.

How much more clearly could God have put the issue? Such is the nature of true repentance, however, that when a couple realize they have transgressed the Scripture, and approach God over the issue in an act of genuine repentance, then I believe the adulterous act of remarriage is absolved in the blood of Christ: 'The blood of Jesus, his Son, purifies us from *every* sin' (1 John 1:7 NIV).

The second step I encouraged them to take was that of sharing with their church the way in which God had spoken to them over the matter. This they did with astonishing results. First, the minister of the church confessed that he believed the Scriptures clearly taught that remarriage was wrong but had been afraid to say so. Secondly, several divorced and remarried couples in the church met to discuss the Scriptures on the subject and came to the same conclusions as the couple I referred to. They too then took the step of repentance, and publicly shared that they had done so. Thirdly, a divorced couple who were planning to be remarried cancelled their wedding plans, and made it clear that they were doing so in the light of the scriptural teaching on the issue. The church I refer to, no stronger than a hundred members, experienced a cleansing influence in their midst that, according to the minister, 'brought the reality of Scripture and its relevance to our lives into greater perspective than any other single event we have known'.

The third step I suggested they should take was that of committing themselves to becoming ambassadors in rebuilding in their community the biblical standards for marriage. Bill Gothard says, 'I believe that one who has experienced a broken marriage has one of the most important messages and ministries in our day: to reinforce scriptural standards on marriage and divorce in the church.' In a booklet on the subject of divorce and remarriage, Gothard tells of one divorced and remarried

couple who, after discovering that they had violated
Scripture, took the step of repentance and confession and
wrote a letter to their minister which they encouraged him
to use when counselling couples who wanted a divorce or
who planned to be remarried. They explained in their
letter how wrong they had been in divorcing and remarrying and that the blessing that was now on their lives was
not God's sanction on what they had done but God's
mercy on their repentant spirit.

Divorced and remarried people, once they realize the
scriptural implications of their position and respond to the
teachings of Scripture in genuine repentance, can, under
God, do as much as anyone to re-establish God's standards
for marriage. One of the greatest needs of these modern
times is for the biblical teaching concerning marriage to
be restored to our churches. I am convinced that the only
way we can stop the rot going any further is by facing up to
these issues of God's word and re-establishing his principles concerning marriage in our Christian communities.

Divorce and the church

There can be little doubt, as we saw in the first chapter,
that the institution of marriage is in serious trouble.
Designed by God to be a lifetime relationship between
two partners, it is breaking apart at the seams. And one of
the most disturbing features of the contemporary Christian
scene is the wrong teaching and counsel on the subject of
divorce and remarriage. We will never stop the slide
towards divorce and remarriage until we stop being
directed by so-called compassion and face up to the clear
teaching of God's word. Of course, people have to be
handled sensitively and compassionately, but let us never
sacrifice the clear standards of Scripture for the sake of
hurting people's feelings. For my own part, whenever I
have confronted a couple who said they wanted a divorce

and said, 'This is not what God wants for you,' I have always done so with tears in my eyes. And in most cases, people have told me that my frankness and loving concern brought them back from the brink of divorce to reconsider the issue in the light of Scripture and to re-establish their marriage on a biblical basis.

While the subject of divorce is regarded as a problem by many, actually it is but a symptom of a much deeper problem—hardness of heart. What was the reason Moses permitted divorce among the Israelites? According to Jesus it was because their hearts were hard (Matthew 19:8). Over the past decade I have noticed that, compared to twenty or thirty years ago, Christians of today are much more resistant to the word of God than they used to be. Is this the result of certain trends in our society? I don't know. But what I do know is that, when counselling Christians today, I notice a hardness that generally speaking was not there a couple of decades ago. When confronted with biblical standards they are more likely to say such things as, 'But God can't love me if he asks me to do that,' or 'This is the only way out.' One man told me recently, 'My case is an exceptional one and is not covered by anything we read in Scripture.'

The problem is not so much divorce, but hardness of heart. And what is the cure for hardness of heart? It is a fresh touch from God—a touch that reaches deep into the personality, re-aligning the will, refocusing the emotions and reconstructing the thoughts. If divorce is a symptom, then there is little point in staying too long with the symptom. Attention must be focused on the root of the problem.

This is why I want to lead you now, in the last chapter, into ways by which you can deepen your spiritual commitment to the Lord Jesus Christ. Based on that commitment, you can discover a love for your partner that you might never have thought possible.

10

WHEN THE WINE RUNS OUT

Remember the famous story of the wedding at Cana of Galilee when the supply of wine ran out? The account is recorded for us in the gospel of John, chapter 2. I have visited the traditional spot where that miracle took place on at least fifteen different occasions. It is one of my favourite stopping places when leading a pilgrimage in the Holy Land, and on that site, I have witnessed scores of married couples recommit themselves to God and each other, following the reading and an exposition of that matchless story in John's gospel.

The account opens with these words: 'There was a marriage in Cana of Galilee.... And both Jesus was called, and his disciples, to the marriage' (verses 1–2). 'God must love a marriage,' said someone, 'because he makes so much of them in his word, the Bible.' The reason for that, I think, is because marriage teaches us more about the nature of the Almighty than perhaps any other human activity.

The Bible both begins and ends with a marriage. It begins with the account of the marriage of Adam and Eve, and ends with the marriage of the bride (this is generally understood to mean the church) to Christ, the heavenly Bridegroom. And the very first miracle Jesus wrought was at a marriage in Cana of Galilee, when he saved a young couple from embarrassment after their supply of wine ran out, by miraculously turning water into wine. They were glad, I'm sure, that they remembered to invite Jesus to their wedding!

The most intriguing point in the whole story of the marriage at Cana of Galilee is, to me at least, the fact that before Jesus performed the miracle of producing wine, he first asked the servants to fill the waterpots with water. Why was this necessary to the divine plan? Could not Jesus have produced wine right there and then in those empty waterpots? I think he could have done; but the reason why he did not do so is brought out best, I feel, by C. S. Lewis in his book entitled *Miracles*.

'The Son can do nothing of himself but what he sees the Father do.' That doctrine, as I understand it, is something like this: there is an activity of God displayed through the creation, a wholesale activity which men refuse to recognize. The miracles done by God incarnate, living as a man in Palestine, perform the very same things as this wholesale activity, but at a different speed and on a smaller scale. God creates the vine and teaches it to draw up water by its roots, and with the aid of the sun, turns that water into juice that will ferment and take on certain qualities. Thus every year God turns water into wine. The miracle of Cana of Galilee will have its full effect on us if, whenever we see a vineyard, we remember that here works He who sat at a wedding party in Cana of Galilee.

Here Lewis is pointing out that whenever Christ worked a miracle on earth, he followed the pattern of his Father in heaven, but on a smaller and speeded-up scale. It takes several seasons for water to become wine by the natural method, but Jesus, by divine power, speeded up the process and produced it in just a moment of time. Lewis also goes on to point out that God, in nature, *begins with what there is* and goes on to increase and multiply it:

Every year God makes a little corn into much corn. The seed is sown and there is an increase. The close-up, the translation of this annual wonder, is the feeding of the five thousand. Bread is not made out of stones, as the devil once suggested to our Lord in vain. A little bread is made into much bread. The Son will do nothing but what he sees the Father do. There is, so to speak, a family style.

So although divine power in Christ could have produced wine in those empty waterpots, our Lord would not do so because it would not be in harmony with the highest laws of the universe. He begins with what is available and proceeds from there to work a most amazing miracle. This, as C. S. Lewis says, is the *family style*.

This insight has particular relevance to what I want to say in this closing chapter, because it may be that in your own marriage, the wine of happiness and true love has run out. You need a miracle. Christ can give you that miracle, but, in doing so, don't expect him to run contrary to the laws of the universe, and suddenly change your feelings and attitudes towards your partner without any effort from yourself. But once, by an action of your will, by commitment and determination, you show God you are willing to do all he asks you, then, and only then, do you position yourself for a miracle. You supply the water and, I promise you, God will turn it into wine.

I am often asked the question: can husbands and wives who have become total strangers ever fall in love again? Is there a way in which a love which has been lost can be recaptured? I believe there is. It is a combination of two things—human effort and divine enabling. Let's look at how it works.

We must begin by examining the three stages of love that are evidenced in human relationships. Richard Strauss in his book *Marriage is for Love* describes these three stages based on the Greek words *eros*, *philia*, and *agape*. *Eros* means sexual love, need love, love that seeks sensual expression. *Philia* means friendship love, companionship love, love that shows concern and care for the other person. *Agape* means unconditional love, self-giving love, love that goes on loving even though the other person becomes unlovable.

Sometimes when I am engaged in counselling a couple prior to marriage I ask them: why do you want to get married to each other? The usual answer is: 'Because we love each other.' Although it would not be tactful at that stage to ask, 'What type of love—*eros, philia* or *agape*?' that is the issue I seek in time to get them to understand. I am convinced that many couples break up because the basis of the 'love' that led to wedding bells was *eros.* And that, in itself, has little staying power. It is interested primarily in what it can get.

It might be helpful now, having introduced you to these three stages of 'love', to look at them in greater detail. Eros (as we said) is sexual love, need love, and it is this type of love that, in most cases, leads to marriage. This is not to say that philia or agape love is not present, but most couples begin their marriage with a preponderance of eros love.

LeRoy Koopman, a marriage guidance counsellor, says that eros is:

—the lingering touch of the fingers

—the deep kiss

—candles and music at dinner

—the 'I promise you' wink

—him giving her a see-through négligé for her birthday

—her wearing it for him the same night

Of course, a certain amount of eros love is necessary in order for a marriage to succeed. It provides the motivation for a couple to relate to each other, touch each other, explore each other and to know each other. Some time after a marriage has taken place, however, the eros, or physical-excitement phase begins to diminish.

Elaine Walster, a professor of sociology and psychology at the University of Wisconsin, USA, interviewed 100,000 people over a period of fifteen years in order to study the differences between 'passionate' and 'compassionate' love. Her studies showed that eros love is short-lived. She claims that for most couples intense passion lasts from six months to about two-and-a-half years. How sad, when eros love diminishes, if there is no philia and agape love to ensure that a marriage functions on a higher level.

Philia love is on a higher plane than eros love because it involves being interested in another person, not for what they can give you, but for what they are. A good word to describe philia love is *companionship*. What is companionship? One writer describes it in this way:

—enjoying each other's company

—reminiscing on the struggles you had to pay your way during the first months and years of marriage

—going shopping together

—sharing breakfast without the morning paper

—turning off the TV to discuss something of mutual interest

—feeling lonely when your partner is away from home on a business trip

—going for a walk together

—washing and drying the dishes together

Philia is a dynamic word, inferring the deliberate overcoming of those forces that work for separation in a marriage. There is enough eros in most marriages to bring people together for a comparatively brief emotional and physical liaison but, sooner or later, if philia love does not ignite, the relationship will grind to a halt.

Agape love is the highest love one can experience in this life or in the life to come. Agape is the way God loves. Anders Nygren, a Greek scholar, has drawn up some parallels between eros and agape which help us to see the nature and meaning of both. According to Nygren, there are three main aspects of agape love:

1. *Agape is spontaneous and unmotivated.* In Christ, there is revealed a divine love which breaks all bounds, refusing to be controlled by the value of its object.

2. *Agape is indifferent to value.* If God, the Holy One, loves the sinner, it cannot be because of his sin; it must be in spite of his sin. But when God's love is shown to the righteous, there is always the risk of our thinking that God loves the person on account of his righteousness or godliness. It is only when all thought of the worthiness of the beloved is abandoned that we can understand what agape is.

3. *Agape is creative.* God does not love that which is already, in itself, worthy of love but, on the contrary, that which in itself has no worth acquires it just by becoming the object of God's love. Agape does not recognize value, it creates it.

Agape love is a commitment of the will in which a person *decides* to love. It is self-giving love, the love that goes on loving even though the other person may be unlovable. This kind of love can revive or resurrect eros love and philia love when they have diminished or died.

I saw this happen recently in the lives of two friends of mine, Alistair and Joan. They came to me with the news that their marriage had 'died', but before moving on to the divorce stage, they felt they owed it to themselves and their family to consult a Christian counsellor, hoping, as they put it, 'that he would confirm our incompatibility'. It was pretty obvious right from the start that there was no eros or philia love left in their marriage. Alistair said, 'I'm not blaming Joan for the predicament we are in because the fault is most certainly mine. But, for some reason, I just don't feel anything for her any more. Whatever existed between us has gone. The spark that brought us together has died.' Joan said, 'This is how I feel, too. It isn't that I have fallen in love with anyone else. What was in my heart towards Alistair the day we were married is no longer there.'

After listening to their story for some time, I said, 'I understand how you both feel, but I'm afraid that my understanding of the Scripture, coupled with my experience, prevents me from confirming your incompatibility. I accept that you have lost the will to make it work. But what I cannot accept is that it should end right there. As you are both committed Christians, I believe God wants you to stay together and make your marriage work....'

'But how can we do that?' broke in Alistair. 'You just can't turn on feelings of love by an act of will.'

'No, that's quite true,' I responded, 'you can't make yourself feel differently just by an act of the will, but what I think you need to discover is that the feelings of romance, and feelings of care and concern, *follow* the doing of the right things. When we begin to do the right thing, the loving thing, towards those we are commanded by God to love (whether we feel like it or not), then God, seeing the commitment of our will and our obedience to his commands, comes to our aid and gives us the feelings.'

'Wait a moment,' said Alistair. 'Do I understand you to say that it is possible for Joan and me to love each other again as we did on our wedding day, by simply following certain procedures?'

'Well, I don't think I would agree with the use of your word "simply",' I responded, 'because the kind of commitment I am talking about is of such a nature that it will mean working hard at what God wants you to do, even though you don't feel like it. But when God sees you are willing to do that, and vote against your feelings, voting instead for him and his word, then he will bring about the change in your feelings. Now if you are willing to give God a chance to renew your marriage by showing him that you are committed to doing what he asks, irrespective of what you may feel about it, then I am willing to work with you and show you some practical steps you can take towards that end.'

Alistair and Joan were silent for a few minutes and appeared somewhat stunned by my words. Eventually Alistair spoke and said, 'I'm willing to try.' Joan took a little longer to make up her mind, but ultimately she too said she was willing. I then took from my files a commitment sheet which I keep for such occasions, and went over it together with them, asking them finally to sign it, thus validating their commitment by so doing.

OUR COMMITMENT

As committed Christians, believing in the authority of the Scriptures and in the power of the Lord Jesus Christ, we together make the following decisions in a spirit of repentance and humility, believing that as we throw ourselves upon the grace and mercy of our Lord, he will enable us to become the people and partners he wants us to be.

WE DECIDE:

1. *To rebuild our relationship and not end it.* Without this decision we know that nothing really will happen. Hopes and wishes are not enough. Our decision is based on the knowledge that God wants us to stay together and make our marriage a reflection of the oneness he enjoys with the Trinity in heaven.

2. *To face the future with patience.* We recognize that the growth between us may at times be painfully slow and that it may be so gradual that it will seem as if nothing is happening. It took time for our marriage to reach the

stage it has and we accept it will take time for it to be rebuilt.

3. *To forgive each other here and now for past failures and mistakes*. We are willing to let go of the bad feelings and memories which have been built up over the past, and to start a clean, new sheet in our relationship. We know that just as God has forgiven us, so we too must forgive each other, and this we do in Jesus' name.

4. *To minister to each other's needs and concentrate on being givers rather than getters in our marriage*. We will endeavour to be sensitive to each other's needs, and attempt each day to do things that bring pleasure to each other, irrespective of whether our needs are met or not. We will especially try to do at least *one* thing each day that will give our partner delight.

5. *To accept responsibility for any hurt feelings we may have, by saying 'I feel' rather than 'you are'*. We realize that projecting blame can damage relationships, and we will seek to build good lines of communication by accepting responsibility for our own personal feelings. We will also seek to share our feelings and not suppress or repress them.

6. *To end each day by praying together and reading Scripture*. We accept that as our spiritual life develops, we will have the resources to handle our human problems with greater insight and understanding, so we will pray and read the Scriptures together daily with the goal of building a deeper relationship with God and with each other.

7. *To establish clear lines of communication and have appointed times for dealing with important issues*. Now that we understand the principles of communication, we will (a) deal with all problems whenever possible on the day they arise, (b) accept responsibility for our own feelings and not project blame on to the other partner, (c) talk through issues until we achieve mutually satisfying resolutions.

Naturally going over the '*Commitment*' point by point

with Alistair and Joan took several hours. Some of the issues needed clarification and called for immediate action. Take point 3, for example, *To forgive each other here and now for past failures and mistakes*. At this point I counselled Alistair and Joan first to ask God's forgiveness for their failures and mistakes, and then to ask each other's forgiveness. I asked them to bow their heads in prayer and individually ask God for his forgiveness. When they had done this, I then suggested that they turn to each other and say, 'Will you forgive me for any hurt I have caused you in our marriage?' I find this to be an electrifying moment when going over the Commitment, for, once forgiveness has been received and given, the personality often experiences a freedom and release that is wonderful to see. I confess I had a lump in my throat when I noticed that as we moved on to point 4, Alistair and Joan were holding hands!

Permit me to focus on another example—point 4—*To minister to each other's needs and concentrate on being givers rather than getters in our marriage*. Here I said to Alistair and Joan, 'Write down some of the things you would like your partner to do for you—things that give you pleasure and add a new dimension to your life together.' After they had done this, I got them to exchange their sheets of paper and then commit themselves to doing one of the things their partner had listed each day of the following week. They were to take them in random order, but focus on doing at least one thing that would bring pleasure to the other.

Before Alistair and Joan left me that evening, I set up an appointment for one week later, explaining that at that time I would not be looking for major changes in their relationship, but simply to see whether they had kept to the rules I had laid down for them. I almost hesitate to begin to go into detail on the next meeting I duly had with them one week later, in case anyone might think that the results I am about to describe invariably happen in this way—because they don't. Sometimes it takes weeks for positive changes in the relationship to begin to emerge, but in Alistair and Joan's case the changes were immediate and dramatic.

As soon as Alistair and Joan sat down in the counselling room, and before I had time to ask them how things had gone, Alistair said, 'If someone had told me two weeks ago that I would be sitting here today wanting to make a go of my marriage, I would not have believed it possible. We did as you said, right down to the letter, and already I am beginning to feel towards Joan the way I felt when I first met her.'

'That goes for me, too,' said Joan. 'Part of me says that this is too good to be true, but I believe, with God's help, this is the answer to our problem.'

Much of that counselling session was taken up with reinforcing what I said in the previous interview—that they were not to concentrate on developing loving feelings for each other, but focus on what they knew God wanted them to do—behave in loving ways. I saw them for several weeks after that, mainly as a point of reference to which they could report. Two months later, Alistair said to me, 'I really don't think we need to come any more. We pray together, read the Scriptures together, have sex together and sort out our problems by following the lines of communication you suggested, so what further need do we have for a counsellor?'

'Fine,' I said, 'all counsellors like to work themselves out of a job. But write to me once a month over the next three months, letting me know how you are getting on. After that there will probably be no need for us to be in touch again, unless, of course, you have something of particular interest to share.'

Alistair did as I asked and kept in touch with me, giving me reports of positive progress. I especially liked the line in his last letter that went, 'Thanks for caring enough to challenge us over the question of divorce. We are working with a couple in our church who are in the same problem that we faced some months ago. I just *know* God is going to use our experience to help them rebuild their marriage in the same way that ours was rebuilt.'

Alistair and Joan's transformed marriage came about through the introduction and application of agape love. What happened in their marriage was this: as they applied agape love—a commitment to do what God wanted them to do even though they didn't feel like it—this gave the Almighty the opportunity he needed to flow into their philia and eros loves, reviving and restoring them, and bringing feeling and romance into their marriage.

There are many marriages in which agape love is not present, and where philia and eros have diminished. When this is so, some couples ask the question: 'Was I ever in love in the first place?' This, however, need not be the pattern for a marriage in which the partners are Christians. If the individuals concerned commit themselves to doing what God asks by demonstrating agape love, then God is able to flow into that marriage and bring about a change in feelings. It is as I said at the beginning of this chapter, a combination of human effort and divine enabling. It is obediently putting the water into the waterpots and then watching the Master turning it into wine. Agape, because it contains the ingredients of God's nature, can keep a marriage going and renew it even when eros and philia are low.

The reality of agape love can best be seen by examining the words of 1 Corinthians 13 in the J.B. Phillips paraphrase, verses 4–8:

> *This love of which I speak is slow to lose patience:* it barricades itself against all irritations and knows how to accept problems and make them work towards further development.

It looks for a way of being constructive: it focuses on the other person and designs ways in which one's partner can be benefited.

It is not possessive: it allows the other person freedom to develop without pressure to conform, without objection and without jealousy.

It is neither anxious to impress: it is secure in its own identity and, because of this, it does not need to draw to itself the positive opinions of others.

nor does it cherish inflated ideas of its own importance: it does not see life as revolving around itself and is, therefore, open to the ideas and suggestions of others.

Love has good manners: having respect for itself, it has respect also for others, and knows instinctively how to do the right thing.

and does not pursue selfish advantage: it does not make its primary concern the satisfaction of personal needs, but has concern for the needs of the other person.

It is not touchy: it is not easily hurt. It does not get too emotionally involved with another's opinions so as to reject the person who gives them.

It does not keep account of evil: it doesn't keep score or continually review and reflect upon the wrongs of a person, but destroys the evidences of past failures and mistakes. It forgives—and forgets.

or gloat over the wickedness of other people: it doesn't use other people's failures to excuse itself.

On the contrary, it shares the joy of those who live by the truth: it is concerned with truth, for without it the universe would fall apart.

Love knows no limit to its endurance: it is able to live with the faults and imperfections of others.

no end to its trust: it goes on believing the best about a person, seeing not merely what the person is but what he can be.

no fading of its hope: it has the assurance that every setback can become a springboard and every stumbling-block a stepping-stone.

It can outlast anything: it goes on loving even when love is not returned.

I remember reading those words from the J. B. Phillips paraphrase many years ago when my own marriage was in the spiritual doldrums, and saying to myself: how can anyone love like *that*? Paul's picture of a love that has 'no limit to its endurance', coming at a time when I did not feel particularly loving towards my wife, raised great problems in my mind. It drove me to cry out: 'Lord, how can I do it?'

As I wrestled with God, I began to realize that God held me responsible to produce not loving feelings in my heart, but loving attitudes. I came to see that the qualities of agape love are not emotional but attitudinal. Emotions may be there, but they are the result rather than the cause of the right attitudes. It slowly began to dawn on me that, in asking me to demonstrate agape love towards my wife, God was not asking me to change how I feel but to change my attitudes. This, of course, demanded a dedicated action of my will. I was unable, simply by an act of choice, to experience loving feelings, but I was able to set my will to see the situation from God's point of view and behave in ways that reinforced that attitude.

Many Christians, I find, have difficulty in accepting the fact that, according to Scripture, man is a responsible being. People tell me over and over again in counselling sessions, 'But I can't do that.' What they are saying, in other words, is, 'I am not able to do what you ask and, therefore, I am not responsible.' We must be clear, as Christians, what it is we can choose and what it is we can't choose. We can't choose to change our feelings but we can choose to change the direction of our will. This is all that God asks. And this is the evidence of agape love.

Of course, it is not as easy as it sounds. As I came face to face with my own personal crisis of loving my wife as God wanted me to, when my feelings were fast diminishing, I went through a period of intense conflict and struggle. My cup of eros and philia love was low, but then I made an act of commitment to God, held up my almost empty cup under the great waterfall of his agape love, and said that I *wanted* to love my wife the way he had commanded me in Ephesians 5:25. He then strengthened my resolve and enabled me to love the agape way. And his agape soon kindled my eros and philia love. I found also that, not only setting my will in the direction the Lord wanted me to go—to love my wife as Christ loved the church—but choosing to act in loving ways (occasionally buying her flowers, taking her out for a meal, helping with the dishes, hanging my clothes up after me, etc.), reinforced my commitment, enabling God to restore to me many of my lost feelings. I did my part—and God did his. The result was that our marriage took on a dimension it never had before—eros, philia *and* agape.

So, if the wine has run out in your marriage, and you believe that the next step is the divorce court—please think again. The one who stepped into a marriage predicament in Cana of Galilee, and rescued it from embarrassment, is with us still. Take the advice of the mother of Jesus who said to the servants: 'Whatever He says to you, do it' (John 2:5 NASB).

> Fill the waterpots with water,
>   Fill them to the very brim.
> He will honour all your trusting,
>   Then leave the miracle to him.
> (*Anonymous*)

Whatever he says to you, do it.

Also in paperback from Kingsway...

A Friend in Need
how to help people through their problems

by Selwyn Hughes

John is unable to overcome his feelings of bitterness and resentment. Anita knows her depression is not physically caused, but she is powerless to do anything about it. Brian is fighting a losing battle with impure thoughts. Like thousands of others in trouble they need to be shown simple scriptural principles that can set them right.

Selwyn Hughes believes that helping people through their problems is not simply the task of ministers and trained counsellors. If you are a Christian, then you are in a position to help others. This book provides guidelines which you can begin to use right away to help people you know overcome their difficulties.

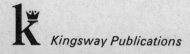

Kingsway Publications

The Christian Counsellor's Pocket Guide

by Selwyn Hughes

Have you ever been asked for help, or confronted with a challenge, only to find that your resources amount to little more than 'I think it says somewhere in the Bible . . .'?

Selwyn Hughes believes that no Christian need find himself in this position, and has therefore compiled this handbook of Bible references and practical advice after many years' experience in the counselling ministry.

Section A deals with the most common problems that trouble Christians;

Section B deals with objections raised by many unbelievers;

Section C confronts the most frequent intellectual excuses given as barriers to personal commitment.

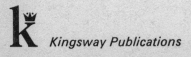

Kingsway Publications

How to Live the Christian Life

by Selwyn Hughes
author of *Every Day with Jesus*

Do you
> *wish the day was over before it has hardly begun?*
> *get irritated by even the smallest problems?*
> *find reading the Bible every day difficult and tiresome?*
> *have trouble mastering temptation?*
> *try to copy others instead of developing your own gifts?*

We can cram our heads with doctrine, but that in itself will not keep us from the problems that rob our lives of the peace, joy and effectiveness that Jesus promised. This book points the way through such problems, helping us to become the kind of people God intended. It is a positive affirmation that we *can* get the best out of the Christian life.

Kingsway Publications

Every Day *Reflections*

by Selwyn Hughes

This collection of daily readings for the whole year covers a wide range of topics to help Christians everywhere on the road to full maturity.

The readings have been selected from *Every Day With Jesus*, the increasingly popular devotional aid released every two months by the Crusade for World Revival.

k *Kingsway Publications*

A New Heart

The promise of God to those who believe

by Selwyn Hughes

Is a victorious Christian life possible?
Can we know power and purity in our
lives, and real faith?

Selwyn Hughes shows how God desires
to win our hearts and so enable us to
turn his promises into reality.

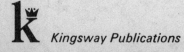

Kingsway Publications

How do you say 'I Love You'?

Expressing Love in Marriage

by Judson Swihart

Many husbands and wives love each other, but have difficulty in communicating that love. They seem to speak different languages. Each one says 'I love you' and hears 'I love you' in a different way.

The author shows how we can use the many languages of love in ways that are meaningful to both partners. He gives practical, down-to-earth suggestions to help us share the love of God as a reality in our homes.

This book has been a great help to us as a couple … There will be few who will not have something to learn from it, and we commend it with confidence and gratitude.

From the Foreword by
Canon Michael Green and his wife Rosemary

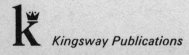

Kingsway Publications